D0378947

ADVANCE PRAISE FOR LIFT

"Bob Vosburgh made the grade as a fighter pilot and in corporate America. Now he has taken time to share his leadership experience with all of us. There are a lot of books on leadership, but none so enjoyable, enthusiastic, and on target. He doesn't preach, he tells stories so you get the idea and retain it."

Charles A. Horner
General, USAF (Retired)
Commander Air Operations Desert Storm

"Bob Vosburgh has written a most readable and enjoyable book based upon the richness of his life's experiences. He shows leadership as a part of our lives, something within each of us, that can be enhanced, nurtured, and applied to making things better. It is important that students understand leadership as a part of life, not just a set of theories with little relevance. Bob accomplishes this through his real-life stories. Every reader will take away a new insight."

Janet Ayres, Ph.D.
Professor, Leadership Development
Purdue University

"A treasure chest of helpful information, based on a wealth of experience and scholarship. This book is a resource that leaders, both young and old, will find extremely helpful."

Merrill A. McPeak
General, USAF (Retired)
Former Chief of Staff, U.S. Air Force

"It is often assumed that leaders are born with skills, and no training is involved. While it is true that leaders are often born with certain talents, they become far more effective with feedback from mentors and experience. Bob Vosburgh's book LIFT *gives the reader the benefit of his, as well as other leaders', experiences. Drawing heavily on his military experiences, he succinctly outlines the elements of leadership. His practical approach addresses many common issues for today's leaders, including key issues of ethics and honesty, that can be applied to a wide variety of organizations and situations, and makes you believe you can 'go above and beyond', as well."*

> **Dr. Jennifer Larsen**
> **Professor and Chief,**
> **Diabetes, Endocrinology and Metabolism**
> **University of Nebraska Medical Center**

"This book could well be named 'Commonsense Experienced Leadership'—it is wonderfully documented, successful leadership at its best. It is leadership for those who aspire to positions of greater responsibility by improving their own performance and that of their subordinates. It is 'Leadership 101' to the tenth power, a compilation of proven ideas, techniques and philosophy."

> **James F. Hollingsworth**
> **Lieutenant General, U.S. Army (Retired)**
> **Highest Decorated General in the History of**
> **the United States, for Valor**

"Bob Vosburgh has written a terrific primer on the essentials of leadership. His relaxed style and candor make every page come alive. He's amplified each point with personal experience from his corporate and military background. LIFT *is a must read for everyone in a leadership position!"*

> **Donald A. Lamontagne**
> **Lieutenant General, USAF**
> **Commander, Air University**

"*Everyone has a teachable point of view and Bob is no exception—except he takes it to the next level! By drawing on his life experiences, Bob has set a standard of measurement for achieving optimum leadership performance. This book is a must read for those leaders who are committed to making a difference!*"

Candace Mailand
National Sales Manager,
Stationary Products Division, 3M Company

"*Bob Vosburgh has written a 'best-seen-to-date' primer on leadership. His commonsense approach and storytelling style make this a most readable book. All readers, young and old, will find approaches that apply to the leadership challenges they face. I highly recommend* LIFT *for every leader's library.*"

Steven R. Polk
Lieutenant General, USAF
Vice Commander, Pacific Air Forces

"*Vosburgh's book is a fresh look at a subject that has been focused upon for centuries. It is particularly interesting in that it has equal applicability to Main Street, Wall Street, and the parade ground. Many old truths are recalled and new angles exposed to observation. It is an easy, fast read that you will enjoy and profit from. IT IS LEADERSHIP AT ITS BEST.*"

Wayne Rollins
Major General, USMC (Retired)
President of the Marine Military Academy
Former Commander of 2nd and 3rd Marine
Expeditionary Forces

"*A skillful blending of leadership lessons and techniques gleaned from successful careers in both the military and commercial worlds. A quick read that will stick to your ribs.*"

Sam W. Westbrook, III
Brigadier General, USAF (Retired)

"We would be much better off if the lessons Bob learned in the Air Force, and passes on in this eminently readable book, were more widely practiced in industry and academia. For that matter, we would be much better off if they were more widely practiced in the military."

Conley Powell, Ph.D.
Fellow, British Interplanetary Society
Advisory Scientist, Technologies Group,
Teledyne Brown Engineering

"Bob Vosburgh's book is an innovative approach to teaching leadership fundamentals. It is a must read for emerging leaders both military and corporate.

"Through statements of experienced and successful leaders personally contacted by Bob, he convincingly portrays important aspects of leadership in a series of situations. Leaders will face related circumstances in pursuit of any profession. These practical examples of effective leadership will bring success to readers as they face related challenges."

Robert F. McDermott
Brigadier General, USAF (Retired)
Chairman Emeritus, USAA

"The title of this book might lead one to think it's a primer on the art and science of flying, but I found it a useful checklist for successfully navigating through life and becoming an effective leader in the process. LIFT indeed gave me a 'lift.'"

Bob Lutz
Chairman, GM North America
General Motors Corporation

LIFT

- To raise in condition, rank or esteem
- To uplift, elate
- To begin flight
- To rise, ascend
- To direct or carry from a lower to a higher position; raise

- *To become elevated; soar*

LIFT

LEADERSHIP THAT SOARS
ABOVE AND BEYOND

Bob Vosburgh

ENTERPRISES, LLC

ISBN 0-9720483-0-8

Library of Congress Catalog Number: 2002_____

Printed in the United States of America

First Printing: April 2002

06 05 04 03 02   6 5 4 3 2 1

99 ENTERPRISES, LLC

to order additional copies of this book, visit www.9gs.org. Quantity discounts available.

CONTENTS

FOREWORD

It is with great confidence and enthusiasm that I recommend this book and its contents to anyone with the need or aspiration to become a more effective leader. The combination of practical lessons, real-life examples and wisdom from both corporate and military leaders makes this an outstanding education for the young leader and a great refresher for those a bit "longer in the tooth."

I first met Bob during the early 1980s when we were both stationed in England, where I was a major general and commander of the 3rd U.S. Air Force in Britain, and he was a young lieutenant. In the twenty years I've known him, I've seen Bob Vosburgh evolve from an eager young fighter pilot to a seasoned leader who applies the lessons of practical experience to the situation at hand, whether in the military or corporate arena.

It was at the Upper Heyford, England, assignment where I first became aware of Bob Vosburgh as I ranked the fighter pilots in the 3rd Air Force. His name repeatedly surfaced to the top of the list. To help you better understand how Bob got to this place in his life, I'll give you a little history.

Bob had two extraordinary parents whose example provided a foundation in ethics, persistence, determination, dedication and perseverance. While I never met his father, I know he was a man of great intellect and common sense. A paraplegic most of Bob's life, his father lived the misfortune of medical complications with a resilience and courage not seen in many human beings.

I do know Robin, Bob's mother. She is a charming Scottish lady whose life experience included three years of Japanese imprisonment as a teenager in Indonesia during World War II. She had an excellent international education, which developed her intellect and prepared her to "press on," irrespective of adversity. Her load was great but she never complained or tired of caring for and exhibiting enduring love beyond imagination for her husband and children. She was a perfect role model, and Bob was an excellent student.

When Bob was thirteen, his father had a stroke, and Bob became the "man of the house." In addition to his considerable responsibilities at home, his parents urged him to participate in a wide array of activities, including athletics, aviation, scouting, travel and his church. This great education, in combination with the complicated home situation, taught Bob to compartmentalize the challenges, look at everything in a positive manner and attack all of his goals in a highly organized fashion.

AS A YOUNG AND EAGER OFFICER

Bob was among the first people I knew who had a complete grasp of modern computers. He volunteered to single-handedly take on the task of writing a computer program that optimized the use of aircraft and aircrews. When installed and instituted, this program proved so effective, a fighter wing rated "Unsatisfactory" was, in record short time, elevated to "Excellent." On his own time and initiative, Bob had taken his academic skills and applied them to a real-world situation, with outstanding results.

Using a Tandy TRS 80 with 16k of memory and an audiocassette tape for storage, Bob wrote a program so impressive that the program and its results were presented to, and adopted by, the senior commanders of the U.S. Air Force in Europe. This incredible staff skill, in combination with his impressive flying skills, had him ranked at the top of the captains and lieutenants in my command. Because of this, I chose Bob to move on to the single slot available for the first ever-operational F-16 assignment in Europe, Hahn AB, Germany.

700-mph fly-by leadership "lesson learned"

Unfortunately, I had to cancel Bob's assignment to Hahn. However, during this time he did learn a valuable lesson in leadership. Young officers rarely understand how their performance(s) affect their immediate supervisors, both positively and negatively. We want pilots to be capable of flying upside down through a hanger or under a bridge, but we also want them to have enough discipline not to do those kinds of things until operationally called upon to do so. "Practice bleeding," here in the form of a 700-mile-per-hour fly-by performed for the benefit of Bob's Scottish relatives, does not produce good results. The Scottish neighbors were not at all pleased.

Because of Bob's action, I had to respond to queries from my boss, his boss, and finally the Ambassador. At each level, I sensed a lack of understanding about why we needed to have extremely enthusiastic, steely-eyed, red-blooded, bulletproof and invincible low-flying fighter pilots. I learned that all of those characteristics, when bundled in Scotland, were called "shining your *arse*." I had to discipline Bob without destroying his career. I think he and I learned a few lessons in leadership; for example, (1) don't put your boss on the spot, and (2) take care of your people. Maybe most of all Bob learned that although we need to stretch the envelope in order to grow, going too far outside the envelope might lead to negative circumstances.

Because I had to cancel his F-16 assignment to Germany, I sent him to be an instructor at Holloman Air Force Base, New Mexico.

HUMBLE PIE ALA MODE

Upon his arrival at Holloman, Bob sought out Colonel Roger Schmitt in charge of flying operations. Bob told him how he had made some mistakes, learned some lessons, and was now intent on being the best instructor that ever happened to the Fighter Lead-In Course. At the end of this tour, Bob was ranked as the top pilot of over 200 instructor pilots. From deep within came a calling to fly the F-16—an assignment he could have landed as he was ranked at the very top of the instructors. However, with his unique combination of flight and academic credentials, he was called upon to teach at the Air Force Academy—an institution he'd revered his entire life. He taught for four years each at Holloman and at the Academy.

Following the tenure at the Air Force Academy, he began his tour in Misawa, Japan. Bob was positioned for rapid future advancement. He had become a flight commander and had again been named a Squadron top gun. Here Bob had to make the gut-wrenching decision of whether to continue on his now on-track career or to be near his father who had been given a terminal diagnosis. He never complained as he moved back to the United States to be near his family. However, Bob was forced to leave flying behind. He was very fortunate to find a job for which he was well equipped: Commandant of Cadets, at Iowa State University. Also, fortunately, it allowed him to be in close proximity to his father whom he cared for diligently.

At Iowa State Bob taught leadership, management, officership, ethics, time management and physical fitness. He was a superb ROTC commandant. He led the cadets on triathlons, took them on trips across the country for valuable exposure to the Air Force and inspired them to higher levels of achievement.

At the end of that assignment, Bob had received a "definitely promote" recommendation to Lieutenant Colonel, but instead continued his commitment to family since his father's condition deteriorated. Bob was offered and accepted an opportunity for an "early-out," since accepting the promotion to Lieutenant Colonel would have required a move away from his father.

From lieutenant to the world of business

Bob moved confidently into the world of finance. At Norwest Investments, he moved quickly up the corporate ladder, demonstrating the confidence, leadership, loyalty, ingenuity and the tireless enthusiasm of a fighter pilot. He found himself in an arena filled with both young and old, all of whom had more experience. He was a principal in the merger of Norwest and Wells Fargo Investments and Insurance. In just five years from the date he signed on as an institutional sales representative, he became head of strategic programs for Norwest Investments and Insurance. Two years later he was the chief executive officer of Online Brokerage Solutions, a startup later acquired by BlueSuit Securities in Chicago. Four months later he was promoted to the chief executive position of BlueSuit and continues to do impressive work.

Bob and I meet frequently, speak regularly and share the joy of hunting and fishing trips. We often discuss management and leadership challenges. I recall one meeting in my hanger in Weslaco, Texas, where we went through a couple hours of leadership quotes and analyzed them. One that comes to mind was from the famous long-time chief of the Air Force Strategic Air Command, Curtis LeMay: "*I simply do not have the time, nor inclination, to distin-*

guish between the incompetent and the unlucky."—a one-sentence lesson in leadership.

When Bob is faced with a significant challenge, he is not the least bit reluctant to pick up the phone and call me. Most often Bob is seeking affirmation for a decision already made, but sometimes we go back to square one and develop new ideas. Here's one: "Most reasonable people, given the same set of facts, will arrive at the same decision." Of course, what comes out of this is:

1) Get the word out so all reasonable people will have the facts.

2) Don't deal with unreasonable people.

I once told Bob our ongoing interaction served to keep my head in the ways of the Air Force, even after my retirement. For the past twenty years, he has also helped to keep me in the vortex of business, as we share our diverse leadership experiences and how they relate to business. I value our friendship, our discussions and the knowledge sharing over the years. You will learn from his advice as I have. Read this book, listen to the lessons and use the book with your staff. Doing so will improve your life, solidify your team and accelerate their performance.

Walter H. (Buz) Baxter
Major General, USAF (Retired)
March 2002

ACKNOWLEDGEMENTS

My father told me that having a strong circle of friends is a blessing. I'm blessed!

First, let me thank some great leaders and fabulous mentors with whom I've had the extreme good fortune to associate. They have provided much of the wisdom you'll find in this book.

Mark Anderson	Neal Barlow
Buz Baxter	Stoney Burke
Hale Burr	Sandra Davis
John Farrish	Dave Fisher
George Harrison	Don Lamontagne
Jim Latham	John Lorber
Randy Mehlin	Jim Paschall
Steve Polk	Dutch Remkes
Jean Schlemmer	Roger Schmitt
Sam Westbrook	Steve Wheeler

I appreciate the support and time spent by the many people who read the documents, looked at cover designs, taught me about writing, helped me with the editing and kept me on track.

Milt Adams	Connie Anderson
Phil Billiam	Marilyn Bleak
Jack Caravela	Duane Deal
Grady Dougless	Mike Frederick
Ed and Gretchen Gilbert	Lowell Grimm
Bill and Judy Hettling	Rick Hoffman
Bob Hudson	John Hyle
Bill Jansen	Ingrid Johnson
Tom Kieffer	Larry Kline
Eric Knutson	Maury and Martha Kramer
Brad Lantz	Mary Lawton
Carol Leach	Walt Lee
Mike Lundborg	Tug McGraw
Scott Mills	Dan and Kathy Moe
Craig Neuzil	John O'Keefe
Shirley Orlofsky	Kevin Perry
Jeff Prouty	Joe Repya
Rex Ridenoure	John Russell
Ray Schwichtenberg	Don Shearer
Sascha Simmons	Joel Spry
Sonja Tepley	Stan Thieman
Lou Tronzo	Kevin Van Voorst
Cathy Veach	Steve Veno
Dell Vosburgh	Robin Vosburgh
Warren Wechsler	Lynn Zigan

I'm indebted to John M. Shanahan for his collection of quotes in *The Most Brilliant Thoughts of All Time*, published in 1999 by HarperCollins Publishers, Inc., New York. I've also found great value in Kenneth Cooper's book *The Aerobics Program for Total Well-Being,* published in 1982 by M. Evans and Company, Inc., New

York, and H. Jackson Brown's book *The Complete Life's Little Instruction Book,* published in 2000 by Rutledge Hill Press, Nashville, Tennessee.

Beyond being understanding throughout this endeavor, I thank my daughter Heather for the many hours of typing transcripts from the videos, my son Blake for his artwork and counsel on design, and my wife Cindy for her help with the many administrative chores associated with the process.

We spent many months traveling, interviewing and video taping the outstanding leaders quoted throughout the book. I could not have finished the task without the talents, expertise and friendship of Steve Goranson. His talents are many, his humor is contagious, and his counsel is wise.

INTRODUCTION

Despite the renewed interest and respect for the military in this country, few corporate executives recognize the quality and value of the leadership training embedded in the military. My personal success in the corporate world is tied directly to that experience.

There are stereotypes of military thinking, leadership and management as slow, outdated, reactionary, heavily bureaucratic and inflexible. This was not my experience. During my fourteen years in the United States Air Force, I worked for high-quality, positively motivating, flexible and selfless individuals from whom I learned much about management, leadership and how to live my life with the proper balance.

I've spent half of my professional life in the military, the other half in the corporate world. My initial impression of the corporate world was corporations manage more than they lead. I believe it still holds true. I'm not saying this is bad news for those of you looking to succeed in your corporate careers. In fact, it is great news because you have the opportunity to be different, lead from the front, motivate your team, derive above-average results from your employees, and enjoy all of the rewards associated with building a superb team.

"I am more afraid of an army of one hundred sheep led by a lion than an army of one hundred lions led by a sheep."
Charles Maurice, 1754–1838

My experience in the Air Force started with leadership training, which took precedence even over technical training. Continuing education focused on communication and excellence. Those with an aptitude for leadership were provided all the necessary training and support. The resources and magnitude of many military situations provides a superb training ground for the future military leaders as well as those who leave the military and become part of corporate America.

Today's Air Force operates under the following three core values: ***Integrity First, Service Before Self, and Excellence In All We Do.*** These values keep it simple and yet, as we'll discuss in more detail, provide all of the guidance one needs to succeed as an officer, a corporate leader, or a citizen.

Think about your current role, military or corporate, in the context of these values. Think of leaders who exude integrity and those (many now removed from office) who haven't. Think of the finest leader you ever worked for. Did they put themselves first, taking credit along the way, or focus on vision, strategy and empowering the team? Finally, I always go back to my father, whose mantra was "If it is worth doing at all, it is worth doing well—Excellence In All We Do."

I went through quite an adjustment when I first moved to the corporate world. I found (and still find) disorganized structure;

compensation and reward systems not tied to a company vision; and managers not willing to motivate, communicate, hold accountable, drive the vision or build a team. I don't blame this on the individuals who have been put into positions of responsibility, but rather on a lack of training and assignment of value to the leadership sector.

My intent is to share with you the best of leadership values I've gathered and tested in the military and during my corporate tenure. The values I learned in the military and as a fighter pilot have served me well in the corporate world. The experience I've had in the corporate world has both validated and expanded the application of the values I've come to rely on. I have watched, listened and learned. I worked hard, challenged the system and had the courage to make the tough decisions. I have a refined set of leadership values we'll talk about in this book. You can benefit significantly if you understand the concepts and have the courage to apply them in your daily work.

The advice given in this book is built upon, and derived from, the careers and accomplishments of many outstanding individuals. Most of my leadership role models come from the military world; many are now firmly entrenched in corporate America, all with significant success.

You can learn from their wins and losses, their time-tested leadership values. Throughout the book you'll find their thoughts. They have all been very supportive of my efforts to put their thoughts into writing. Many took time for a full-fledged interview—others responded to my queries in a written format. In any case, the anecdotal support and specific examples they provide are of great value. You'll find their biographies at the end of the book.

If you've decided to spend your life being a corporate drone, hoping for a stable economy, planning on retirement so you can just fade away, staying out of the vortex, and not challenging the status quo—this book is not for you.

If you want to make a difference, gain the respect of those you work for and those who work for you, if you want to take your team to a performance level completely out of the corporate paradigm, then read on.

In 1979, I was off to England for my first operational assignment. I met a group of leaders there who have influenced my life and my leadership style for more than twenty years.

Sam Westbrook, top of his class at the Air Force Academy and a Rhodes Scholar, went on to attain the rank of major general before he retired. John Lorber earned four stars and commanded the entire U.S. Air Force in the Pacific. Tony McPeak went on to become a four-star general, Chief of Staff of the Air Force. Don Lamontagne is a three-star general, and heads up what the Air Force calls Air University. Dave MacGhee is a two-star general, and oversees the Air Force Doctrine Center. Steve Polk is a three-star general, vice commander of the Pacific Air Forces.

In the Air Force the odds of becoming a general officer are well under 1 percent. With approximately 100 fighter pilots at that assignment, you can see the environment was unique, the examples set were superb, and the accomplishments associated with that particular group incredible. At the time, their boss was Major General Buz Baxter. General Baxter has had more influence on my professional and personal life than any other mentor. I've carried the lessons of these individuals across the line between the military and corporate worlds. We'll share lessons from all of them throughout the book.

Throughout my trek I've picked up *best practices* from mentors, leaders and peers. I've studied and taught management and leadership. I've been able to apply the combination of those factors in both military and corporate environments. Hard work and some luck sent me to fighter assignments with an incredible concentration of outstanding leaders. I've worked for the good and the mediocre, the best and what felt like the worst, the teachers and the politicians, the suck-ups and the selfless. In this book I will share with you how the training and experience of the military, peppered with the reality of the corporate world, has led to nine values I rely upon in my daily leadership challenges. As a result, I have plenty of examples to illustrate three important components of leadership: self, team, and atmosphere. Within those components I'll highlight nine specific areas:

1. Excellence
2. Mentors
3. Balance
4. Clarity
5. Hiring, Firing and Empowerment
6. Ensuring Accountability
7. Positive Thinking
8. Giving Credit
9. Generating Enthusiasm

THE FIRST OF THE THREE SECTIONS IN THIS BOOK WILL FOCUS ON SELF

We need to look at how important it is for us to set a standard of excellence and diligence in all we do, improve ourselves via mentors and do it with stamina and balance. F-16 pilots work six or seven days per week. We studied, we practiced and we exercised. We were the leading edge, with the finest equipment, and we were always well prepared. In order to maintain the intensity, we needed contrast and balance. We socialized on Friday nights, but you'd find us running five miles on Saturday and spending some time together. Weekends may have included trips to the squadron vault to study classified materials, but also included plenty of time with family and friends.

We can't do our best if we aren't our best. You need to achieve your optimum physical, mental and emotional balance to function as an effective and inspirational leader. Physical fitness, diet and rest really do make a difference. I relate this not to the Peter Principle, but what is called the Paul Principle. The Paul Principle suggests that by the time a person gets to a significant leadership/management opportunity, they are too burned out to be effective. Have you noticed those around you who have already shut down, who focus on the end of the workday and early retirement? Our bodies and minds need to be exercised and challenged to maintain the vitality to lead and motivate. We need to find an emotional/attitude balance that takes us through the stressful and trying times. We need to have a mindset that helps us carry on, treat people properly, accept both the strengths and weaknesses of our team and focus on the present to find maximum effectiveness.

THE SECOND OF THE THREE SECTIONS OF THIS BOOK WILL FOCUS ON TEAM

The year 2001 was one of the most significantly challenging times in our history. It started with tough times for the economy, nearly impossible conditions for the financial services industry, and then the most devastating event I can remember on September 11. The destruction of the World Trade Center knocked us all down a notch. People returned to fundamentals; they turned to their families, they turned to their faith, and they fought to keep their jobs. The call for effective leadership has never been louder. How do you bring your team to focus on the vision and strategy of the business? How do you create an environment that provides the support that team members need to maintain the proper balance to carry on in even the most stressful times?

A group of employees is nothing more than a draw upon resources if they don't function as a team. A team functions well if it has a clear vision of where it is going, if credit is given to the proper employees and if the top performers are empowered to make a difference.

General John Lorber, formerly commander of the U.S. Air Forces of the Pacific, and currently a senior executive with Boeing, gives an example of a runway repair team that worked for him in Misawa, Japan.

JOHN LORBER—VICE PRESIDENT, BOEING SPACE AND COMMUNICATIONS OPERATIONS AND RETIRED GENERAL: *We busted the first Operational Readiness Inspection (ORI), horribly. We weren't ready. There were a lot of reasons we could have given, but there was no excuse for not being ready. One new leader, John Estes, was brought in to improve the civil engineering team. He started every workday with a team run; they practiced constantly, they performed their tasks in less time than was required, they worked together, they lived together, they excelled together. When the evaluation team made its next visit, one snowy morning at 2 A.M., the runway repair team was put into action to repair some simulated craters. They finished it in a record time of one hour, 58 minutes.*

Then, John Estes got his bulldozers out there and started digging some more holes, and they started their repair process on those simulated bomb craters. The inspection team said, "You don't have to do this, the inspection is over." And he said, " I want to show you what we really can do." So he had the team all fired up.

I remember being out there at two o'clock in the morning watching them, and trying to help out. Before long, I bet half the wing was out there, most of the people not able to provide assistance, but they were cheering. When they finished, the cheer I heard was as loud as I've ever heard in any sporting event. They had scored, and they had won. The leader was inspiring, the team was pre-

pared, the atmosphere was contagious and the goals were not only met but exceeded.

Managers are different creatures than leaders

A leader inspires the team to follow them up the hill into adversity. A manager counts numbers, follows metrics and makes widgets. A well-led team will make more widgets!

An effective leader compels teamwork and comaradery, mutual support and enthusiasm, accountability and recognition. An effective leader gets above-average performance out of the team.

THE LAST OF THE THREE SECTIONS OF THIS BOOK WILL FOCUS ON ATMOSPHERE

Why die all tensed up? It has been documented that working in a positive atmosphere is preferable to working in a negative (fear, sarcasm and ridicule) environment—preferable for both morale and results. A positive environment creates the momentum and attitude we need to get through the tough times.

I once worked for a general who said he utilized two simple tests when visiting divisions of his command. First, he looked for smiling faces, enthusiastic attitudes and positive momentum. Absence of these characteristics was a leading indicator that the unit would not perform well. Second, he watched for commanders who gave subordinates the opportunity to share their stories. If the commander spent all his time "tooting his horn," then the unit was bound to be less effective. Giving credit to subordinates and empowering them to share successes with top brass is a characteristic of strong team environment.

The team needs to carry an enthusiasm for the tasks at hand to be truly outstanding. Have fun, raise the bar and celebrate every victory. Team events, reward and recognition programs and spontaneous celebrations should be common. Use sprints and longer drives in combination, but ensure that short-term wins can be utilized to energize the group. Walk around, give immediate recognition and tie rewards to specific milestones.

CHAPTER ORGANIZATION AND STRUCTURE

Throughout the book I'll be quoting people I've learned from. I learned early on in my teaching roles that examples and specific experiences are the keys to retention. You can expect a combination of stories from personal experiences and quotes of wisdom from successful leaders.

> *"Mentoring isn't about the transfer of information but of wisdom."*
> ### Jean Schlemmer,
> ### Corporate Executive

For those unfamiliar with rank in the military, it goes something like this:

- 2nd Lieutenant
- 1st Lieutenant
- Captain
- Major
- Lieutenant Colonel
- Colonel
- Brigadier General ★
- Major General ★★
- Lieutenant General ★★★
- General ★★★★

I had the great fortune to attend the Air Force Squadron Officer's School. At the time, the school was saved for the top quarter of eligible captains. There I learned most any form of communication could be organized by starting with three main points. If you need to expand upon it, add three sub-points to each of the three main points, and so on. You'll note I have three main sections, with three chapters in each. Hey, works for me!

I'll attempt to summarize what I consider the most important three points at the end of each chapter. On to Chapter 1 and Excellence.

SELF

In this section, focused on self, we'll look at:
- Excellence,
- Mentors, and
- Balance.

1

EXCELLENCE

Since we're talking about excellence as it relates to self, I'd like to touch upon three areas we have some control over.

- Excellence in our daily activities,
- Excellence as it relates to integrity, and
- The difference between striving for excellence and for perfection.

EXCELLENCE IN OUR DAILY ACTIVITIES

Roger Carr was a 1964 graduate of Iowa State University who died in an aircraft accident at Eglin Air Force Base, Florida, in January 1966. While at Iowa State, Lieutenant Carr served as a Cadet Group Commander during his senior year. When he graduated from Air Force pilot training in August 1965, he was named top pilot graduate of the year in Air Training Command. The

Daily Activities

Integrity

Excellence versus Perfection

words engraved on his memorial plaque are the words he lived by and the advice he constantly gave the Cadet Corps while he was Cadet Commander.

"Whatever you do, if it is worth doing,
it is worth doing well."

An award in his honor recognizes the senior cadet considered to have the most potential for achieving the standard of excellence demonstrated by Lieutenant Carr as an Air Force officer and as a pilot.

I received this award in 1976 and have done my best to live up to its message. If you think about it, what sense is there in going into any profession with the goal of simply hanging on, staying in the background or making the fewest waves? We have but one lifetime to add value and make a difference.

The thought of living one's life by this mantra can be a bit overwhelming. However, if one is able to compartmentalize and deal with it just one day at a time, it is very doable.

BUZ BAXTER—BUSINESSMAN, FIGHTER PILOT AND RETIRED MAJOR GENERAL: *When undertaking a task/mission/job you must, before it ever comes up, decide what you will NOT compromise about. On issues of importance, establish a written list of things you will not permit "on your watch." Keep it current. Live by it. Don't permit yourself to become a "damage control officer." RETIRE/QUIT before you compromise.*

I remember hearing a story about Dr. Henry Kissinger. He had passed a project on to some of his staff and, after some time, they brought a report back to him for review. A few hours later he called the project lead and asked, "Is this the best you can do?" The project lead went back to work on the assignment and in due time dropped another report off for Dr. Kissinger's review. Once again,

Dr. Kissinger asked, "Is this the very best you and your team can do?" The project lead answered, "Yes, it is!" Dr. Kissinger then replied, "O.K., now I'll read it."

HALE BURR—CONSULTANT, FIGHTER PILOT AND RETIRED MAJOR GENERAL: *It is important that leaders are technically competent in their "core business," whether it's flying jet fighters or selling investments. The spectrum of broad-based experience as the best teacher and training in the field are the most suitable career path backgrounds. It is necessary for credibility to understand the military mission or specific purpose of whatever business activity you are involved in when communicating to followers.*

It is common for our team members to approach their roles in a way less than optimum for overall team productivity and effectiveness. Imagine if every single team member always took their tasks to be so important they'd ensure a level of excellence beyond reproach. What if everyone in the organization questioned all actions as Dr. Kissinger questioned his staff? I think it would be immensely positive.

HALE BURR—CONSULTANT, FIGHTER PILOT AND RETIRED MAJOR GENERAL: *One of the lessons I had learned very early in my Air Force career was to work my bosses problems and not my own! I served under a number of bosses who had a reputation of being very difficult to work for. As an F-15 Squadron Commander and Director of Operations I found out and applied the best approach for dealing with really tough guys (who would fire you in a heartbeat and had a history of leaving numerous "dead bodies" behind them in each assignment). Simply put, don't avoid the problems that always arise in large complex organizations. Roll up your sleeves* *and get your hands dirty wrestling with the issues. Tell your boss what's wrong, how you're going to fix it and when it will be corrected.*

General Tony McPeak, former Chief of Staff of the Air Force, once told me he never asked for a specific assignment in the Air Force. He did his best at whatever job he was given. Whether in a bunker in Germany or flying the F-100 as a U.S. Air Force Thunderbird, he did his best at that job on that day. He shared this with me when he was a colonel; fifteen years later he was commander of the entire Air Force.

HALE BURR—CONSULTANT, FIGHTER PILOT AND RETIRED MAJOR GENERAL: *Life is too short to experience everything. I think continual structured reading that helps you grow is extremely important. You can learn a lot from people who are proven winners in their field of endeavor. One also needs to learn from the mistakes of others so as not to repeat them. To keep your composure under stress, it helps to know that others have faced difficult circumstances and survived.*

You cannot expect this sort of behavior out of your senior staff, your direct reports, if you don't "walk the talk." If you share with your team that you owe a report to your superiors and you are going to simply "pencil whip" a quick response and move on . . . expect the same sort of behavior from your team when you ask for high performance.

DUTCH REMKES, FIGHTER PILOT AND AIR FORCE BRIGADIER GENERAL: *I ask folks to also select a personal value and try to connect it to the organization's value system. The one I have chosen for myself is humility.*

As a lieutenant, in England, I worked for then-Colonel Sam Westbrook. We had a set of bureaucratically designed training requirements intended to keep us combat ready, but instead kept us focused on "filling squares" rather than the more important aspects of our mission. Those requirements were reinforced by the evaluation system for our superiors, who looked at metrics and percentages associated with their teams and how many of the training squares were completed. Fighter squadron commanders spent a lot of time looking at how the squares were being filled versus how ready we were for combat. Colonel Westbrook had the courage to stand up to that particular system, suggest we focus on the mission at hand, let the numbers fall as they may, and then take any opportunities provided by those results to challenge and improve the system. He was, and continues to be, a great example of excellence in leadership.

"Only dead fish swim with the stream."
Anonymous

I feel strongly that courage is a core component of effective leadership. Challenge the absurd, do the right thing.

Put yourself in the shoes of your superiors and imagine one of your subordinates coming to you and challenging a system that is making the company or team less efficient and less productive. Would you throw them out the door? Of course not! Speak up, be counted and make a difference.

In my very next assignment, I had the opportunity to practice the standard set for me by Colonel Westbrook. Holloman Air Force

Base in New Mexico had about 200 instructors who taught new fighter pilots the basics of air-to-air and air-to-ground combat. It was a fabulous assignment where we'd fly two to three times every day in the AT-38, a fun, supersonic trainer. The problem was we were spread pretty thin and ended up doing paperwork on the weekends. And as a result of this and the fact the weather was always clear in New Mexico, we didn't get all of the "bad weather" training requirements accomplished on a timely basis. The aforementioned system that had been improved in England hadn't yet made it to the United States.

I worked for a squadron commander who was a "square tracker" and who pointed out to me that I hadn't completed the required practice instrument approaches. I told him I'd do my best, but I'd need a dedicated flight to finish those approaches. The schedule was so busy the dedicated flight wasn't made available, and as we approached the end of the month, I still hadn't finished the required instrument approaches. I walked by the computer printout and looked to verify the shortcoming. To my great surprise, I noticed I was completely finished with all the required training events!

When I asked the appropriate people how this could have occurred, I ended up in front of the squadron commander who "dressed me down" and suggested I let the issue go. Here I was a captain, and this lieutenant colonel was telling me to ignore the fact the numbers had been falsified. Questions: "What were they going to do, send me to work for a commander I didn't trust?" I was already in that situation. "What were they going to do, turn me in for being honest?" Well, I said I would not tolerate this and went back to have the numbers changed. The squadron commander, not the brightest light in the chandelier, decided he'd take this issue to his boss. His boss was Colonel Roger Schmitt, an outstanding individual and a high-integrity fighter pilot. It didn't fare so well for the squadron commander!

On the other hand, shortly thereafter, I was selected to be a Standards and Evaluation Check Pilot. Six of some 200 instructors were selected for this role, which included giving check rides, determining pilot qualification and instructor proficiency for the entire cadre. The instructor pilots were ranked from 1 to 200; I left ranked #1. Although there was some pain associated with making the proper choice, I battled through it, took the heat from my boss for not falsifying forms, and I ended up a better person for my actions. I also feel confident the standard accepted by the other instructor pilots was elevated. So, "What are they going to do to you?" Well, they are going to recognize you as a better person, rank you higher for promotion and assignment and recognize your integrity.

EXCELLENCE AS IT RELATES TO INTEGRITY

MARK ANDERSON—CONSULTANT, FIGHTER PILOT AND RETIRED LIEUTENANT GENERAL: *If you're emphasizing "self" in these three points, the most critical "must have" in my opinion, is INTEGRITY. Without it, trust, confidence and credibility go out the window—and are nearly impossible to recover.*

As a set of guidelines, the three core values established by the Air Force Academy in the early '90s, and subsequently adopted by the Air Force, are as good as any I've seen:

"Integrity first, service before self,
and excellence in all we do"

I'm telling you straight: I've told a fib or two in my time. I remember my mother coming after me with a bar of soap to wash my mouth out for lying to her. I've spent some time in "circumlocution"—better known as beating around the bush or avoiding the truth—so as to avoid an admission of guilt in front of people I knew would lose respect for me. But I'll also tell you I've improved to the point where I now do my best to tell it like it is, wear my heart on my sleeve, and understand that being honest is, in fact, the best policy. Continuous improvement and doing all we can to reach acceptable standards is about all we can ask and strive for as leaders.

RANDY MEHLIN—AIRLINE PILOT, FIGHTER PILOT AND RETIRED LIEUTENANT COLONEL: *The boss must be honest and aboveboard always—not only when it's convenient or the best thing for the boss. Don't hesitate to acknowledge your own screw-ups. It can foster an attitude that this is not a one-mistake outfit. There are always lessons to be learned. Don't be afraid to let others fail. I always wanted to know the boss would watch my back if I was trying to go in the right direction. Above all, don't look for excuses/scapegoats or tolerate those who do. Suck it up! Don't let mourning our losses/mistakes/shortcomings become more prevalent than celebrating our success.*

I remember the cross-examination I had to undergo in my quest to become an Eagle Scout. I had studied very hard for the exam, read all of the books and memorized to the best of my ability. As I went through the examination, I was led to some questions I really had no hope of answering. I responded to these honestly saying, "I don't know the answer to that question, sir." By the time I left the room, I was certain I'd failed the test, knowing I'd missed some of the questions. However, when I was called back into the room, I was congratulated for passing the test with flying colors. Turns out this particular board purposely took all candidates to the point where they couldn't answer the questions. The goal, of course, was to test the integrity of the candidate. Lesson learned.

DAVID FISHER—BUSINESSMAN, FINANCIAL CONSULTANT AND ENTREPRENEUR: *I think integrity is essential to every area of life. It's commonly said that integrity is what we do when no one is looking. When we conduct ourselves with integrity—that is, honestly, forthrightly, with a determination to pursue righteousness—I think it shows in ways that we don't realize. We stand taller, we conduct ourselves with great confidence, and we look at people in the eyes . . . it's in our very ethos. But if we're dishonest, people WILL see it. They might not see the particular event where you were dishonest or acted in a low-integrity manner, but they will sense it.*

The value of integrity was reinforced when I was teaching ethics to cadets at the Air Force Academy. It was just a couple of lessons each semester, but I remember standing in front of them, going by the course script, and realizing what a fabulous environment we would have if we knew everything communicated was true and accurate.

JIM PASCHALL—RANCHER, BUSINESSMAN, FIGHTER PILOT AND RETIRED LIEUTENANT COLONEL: *I think no trait is worthier than being honest. Shading events in order to make them appear more attractive has gotten more leaders in trouble than any other activity I know. It may work in the short haul, but sooner or later that tactic will come back to haunt the leader.*

It is not possible to run a high-performance team if we are not of the highest integrity. Why? We have to trust everyone who reports to us, and that isn't possible if they can't trust us.

I have a humorous example of an incredibly low-integrity individual who reported to me at Norwest Corporation. It was laughable the way he would contrive stories to justify poor performance, the way he would falsify reports and trump up his unit's productivity. A friend of mine suggested he was so bad he would say just about anything to avoid confrontation or any indication he wasn't "with the beat" of our organization. One day, we stood at my office window and were discussing how we might do a campaign involving the use of billboards throughout the Seattle and Atlanta areas. I asked this individual if he could see the red billboard several blocks away. No billboard actually existed. He stuttered a bit while we stood quietly, and finally said, "Oh, the red one, yes I see it now, my eyes aren't what they used to be." Now I'm not saying this is commonplace, nor am I saying you should attempt this baiting technique with your team. I am, however, absolutely amazed anyone would find benefit or expect anything positive to come out of such a petty lie. People like this shouldn't be retained, and we didn't retain them!

You cannot accept anything less than integrity from your team. A violation of integrity is a warning of more to come. Eliminate the threat to you, your business and the team and help them find someplace else to work. Keep a clean team.

THE DIFFERENCE BETWEEN STRIVING FOR EXCELLENCE AND FOR PERFECTION

BUZ BAXTER—BUSINESSMAN, FIGHTER PILOT AND RETIRED MAJOR GENERAL: *Strive for excellence, but recognize there is a difference between that and perfection. My British boss at AFNorth, General Sir Anthony Fara-Hockley, frequently used the expression: "Perfection is the enemy of the Good." When time is a principal factor, "Good" is always better than "nuthin."*

When I was with Norwest Corporation, I was fortunate to go through a leadership course entitled "Leadership & Mastery." During that course we spent an afternoon with CEO Dick Kovacevich, who shared his thoughts about being an excellent company. One of his comments related to the reinvention process and how we could evolve with efficiency and, at the same time, stay ahead of the competition and deliver excellent products. I'll paraphrase, "There is no need for us to reinvent any wheels, no need to start from scratch. It is a much more effective process to evaluate the landscape, take some ideas that seem to have merit, tailor them to our needs and look for continuous improvement. Pride of authorship can be very ineffective. Giving others credit and learning from their example can be very effective. Moving forward with a concept not totally refined is usually better than spending our lives at perfecting a new product line, never getting it to market."

My company is in a continuous process of reinvention, seeking excellence in what we deliver and looking for a compatible sector of the marketplace. At the beginning of every year, we go through a three-month process of reinvention.

"It wasn't raining when Noah built the ark."
Howard Ruff

Specifically, I mix up the company divisions for the sake of diversity and perspective, and then create multiple reinvention teams. The teams start by reading and doing research on the financial services industry. They search out strategic thinkers and research on the future of banking, brokerage, retirement and insurance. They bring this together so as to define a map of the next several years. A lot of people spend money on research and predicting the future. Thanks to them for spending the money, taking the time, saving the day and providing the information we need to find continuous improvement.

Once the map has been constructed, it is time to look at our resources, as if we are building a new company from scratch, to determine which part of the terrain is the best fit. If it is in the insurance business because of strategic partners or talent in the ranks, so be it! What are the new products we'll need to provide for a competitive advantage three years from now? Let's boil those down to the three to five we find the most attractive and dig down into the details of how, when, why and what the market opportunities are likely to support. Independently, each of the teams takes those products and builds a business case for restructuring the company.

At the end of the three-month exercise, we have an offsite meeting where the new business models are presented. As a team we take all ideas and select those products and services that are overwhelmingly the most popular and profitable for our company. We've then developed our vision for the next year, the products, the support, the strategy and the roadmap we'll follow so we can "join the sigmoid curves." If you've not heard that term, let me illustrate.

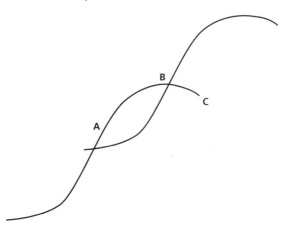

A business product offering can be looked at much like a sigmoid curve. In the illustration above, you can see how a sigmoid curve shows early, mid and mature growth for a new product. The development and adoption stage (A), the mature/leveling off stage (B) and the decline/end of the cycle (C). For our company to continue to grow, year after year, cycle after cycle, we must learn to "join the sigmoid curves." By the time one product offering gets to the mature/leveling off point, we should be well along the path of overlaying another product set so a new sigmoid curve can be intercepted.

It is all about continuous improvement, excellence on a daily basis and reinvention. Overriding this process, however, is the need to get products out to the street, to deliver a marketable product and to generate revenues. A company that lives for strategic planning at the expense of execution will have a hard time surviving in today's short and aggressive business cycle. Sometimes it all boils down to having the energy and drive to make things happen.

As a young pilot flying the F-111 fighter, I had relatively low flying hours compared to the more senior cadre in my squadron. Several of us lieutenants looked for ways to build our flying time and experience. I was always ready to fly, and I spent time every day checking in with the squadron schedulers, letting them know I was available should anyone be ill or should they need another pilot. I ended up with significantly higher flying hours in my first year than others because I was always prepared when the opportunity presented itself. I wanted my commanders to know if they needed a pilot, all they had to do was turn around and I'd be standing there. I was ready to take advantage of any opportunity that presented itself, and my bosses knew it. Part of excellence in our daily activities is being prepared for and anxious to find those opportunities.

The F-111 was one of the more challenging aircraft because of the complexity of its systems. It flew fast, it flew slowly and the wings swept. The inlet geometry for the engine was variable, the radar modes, the bombing modes, the hydraulic systems, the fuel system, the electrical system and life support systems were complex. I didn't want to simply understand the systems as well as the average F-111 pilot, I wanted to know them better than anyone else at Upper Heyford, England. I wrote a master question file (MQF) of some 720 questions that asked every question about every system. I got to where I could answer every one of those questions, from relief valve pressures, to weapons delivery options, to electrical circuit specifics. The Vosburgh MQF was still in use by the training squadrons a decade after I left the airplane.

Extra work, sure. Less time with the family, absolutely. Less time at the bar, of course. But was I doing my best with the job I was assigned? Yes. Remember, "Whatever you do, if it is worth doing, it is worth doing well." I ended up using the same technique, outlining the technical manuals, finding the most critical pieces of information, turning them into questions and then studying them routinely for other flying assignments in the future. This extra effort and going beyond the expectations of my peers and bosses made a difference.

I wanted to understand the bombing geometry better than anyone else in my flying squadron. It is a complex set of variables that today are greatly simplified by computers, radar ranging and other technology improvements. In the manual world of dropping bombs, there are many considerations: alignment with the target, airspeed, dive angle, ordinance type, altitude and correction for the winds. Rolling in on the target while trying to dive at precisely 20 degrees, while attempting to set the power so you are at precisely 480 knots, taking your best guess at the winds, trying to find the target, looking for the proper offset aim point, and pushing the bomb release button at the right time is a challenge. Part of the challenge was getting enough practice time to refine the process. Learning to correct the release point for discrepancies in airspeed, altitude, dive angle or any combination of the three was challenging. The combination of tasks was so saturating, in fact, many a fighter pilot has perished over the years trying to figure out the right time to release the bombs, flying right into the ground with what is called "target fixation."

In 1979, I had one of the early personal computers, a TRS-80 Model I. It had 16k of RAM, a Z80 processor, and programs were stored on an audiocassette tape. The monitor was black and white and very crude. Despite that, I wrote a program that simulated a dive-bomb pattern. It would randomly generate airspeeds and dive angles and put the operator on a flight path towards the target. The user had to quickly compute the correction for the airspeed error and the dive angle error, figure a new bomb release altitude, and then drop the bomb at the appropriate altitude. I programmed it so two people would play "the game." We set it up on the alert pad, a delightful place where we would live for many days at a time, waiting for WW III. The computer was used constantly; the pilots loved the competition and, more important, we all became better at quickly computing the proper bombing solutions. Many people improved their bomb scores based on that little program and the solution presented. Just one more example of putting in the extra effort for the sake of excellence. Today, of course, there are plenty of simulators with very realistic depictions of flight conditions. Also, the systems on the newer aircraft have taken the bombing accuracy to much better CEAs (circular error averages).

NEAL BARLOW—PROFESSOR, AIR FORCE PILOT AND COLONEL: *Excellence is very important in developing strong organizations. If you do not have integrity, your subordinates will not trust you. They will know while you may say one thing, you may actually do something else. If we fail to show excellence, why would we expect any of our subordinates to show excellence in what they do? If an organization is going to be successful, the leader needs to be willing to adhere to high standards at all times, not only when it's convenient.*

It is the extra effort, and what we can do above and beyond expectations, that define excellence in effort.

ROGER SCHMITT—BUSINESSMAN, FIGHTER PILOT AND RETIRED COLONEL: *Any organization that strives for less than excellence will eventually fail. Not always easy to achieve, it must start at the top and be communicated effectively to all. You must practice what you preach. I've always been a believer in the "let me show* *you how this is done," approach rather than "I told you what I expect/want now, go do it."*

I promised you three main points. Here is a recap:
- Excellence in our daily activities,
- Excellence as it relates to integrity, and
- The difference between striving for excellence and for perfection.

2

MENTORS

Over the years I've decided it is easier to learn from an outstanding leader than to make it up as you go. The value of a mentor can be derived in person, over the phone, over the Internet, or by simply picturing their presence. You should find one, or many mentors, or perhaps they'll select you, but make sure they have a style you can emulate.

- Learn from outstanding leaders.
- Picture their presence.
- Find a style you can emulate.

LEARN FROM OUTSTANDING LEADERS

RANDY MEHLIN—AIRLINE PILOT, FIGHTER PILOT AND RETIRED LIEUTENANT COLONEL: *If I had to pick the common thread of the best*

Learn from Leaders

Picture Their Presence

Find a Style

leaders I've known, I would lean toward attitude. Does he believe in the job/mission statement and like working with people? Is he positive, upbeat? One of my mentors always told us our most important job was to train our own replacement.

Peacetime is full of contradictions for a young fighter pilot. On the one hand we're trained to fly on the deck (this means close to the ground) as fast as the airplane will go to avoid enemy radar. We aggressively pull the aircraft to 45 degrees nose high, roll over on our backs, find the target and enter a dive bomb pattern. We drop the bombs, pull away at four times the acceleration of gravity and then reenter the low-level flight environment while leaving the target area as fast as possible. On the other hand, we are to comply with training regulations, never go below minimum altitudes or above maximum airspeeds. We are to ensure we have proper clearance before entering the practice bombing range where we can be fouled for going too low or ignoring proper procedure.

In 1981, I was flying F-111s out of Upper Heyford, England, and quite enjoying the assignment. You may know of the F-111, a swing-wing, supersonic, fighter-bomber. Originally it was designed to be the do-all fighter in the 1960s. Some versions were made to land on aircraft carriers. It was expected to do intercepts as well as drop bombs. The F-111 utilized variable wing sweep so it performed well at both high and low speeds, and it required both a pilot and a weapons systems operator (WSO or navigator) to run the systems.

I was one of the first lieutenants to go directly to the commander's seat of the airplane. The "old heads" at that base were concerned enough with "the youngster" that they ensured I got plenty of flying time to maintain a reasonable proficiency level. It was complex, and I loved it! About halfway into my assignment, I was qualified as a functional check flight pilot (FCF) and got to fly F-111s coming out of maintenance to test the systems. These flights were required before the airplane could be put back on "the line" for squadron pilots. What a blast. We'd climb out at 650 knots and end up around 50,000 feet at about 2.5 times the speed of sound. We'd check all the systems, shut down one engine at a time to ensure they'd restart, bring the jet back home and write up all of the discrepancies. I remember these well; they took me into a flight regime many never saw, and the experience was outstanding. My last flight in the F-111 was with my good friend Lieutenant John Manzi, who went on to fly the SR-71 Blackbird (the highest, fastest, coolest reconnaissance jet ever built), retiring recently as a lieutenant colonel. I often think our last flight, one above 50,000 feet, was great training for his Blackbird assignments.

SAM WESTBROOK—CONSULTANT, BUSINESSMAN, FIGHTER PILOT AND RETIRED BRIGADIER GENERAL: *Different people learn most effectively in different ways, but I certainly think mentors have been very important for me. My high school physics teacher, who pushed us into analytical problem solving and made the connection between mathematics and physical phenomenon, launched me on a pursuit of science. Captain Beau Puryear spent mornings and evenings at the Air Force Academy working with a group of cadets interested in trying for the Rhodes and other post-graduate programs. Win, lose, or draw, everybody who came in contact with*

Beau ended up addicted to policy analysis. An effective mentor chooses to use their time to invest in the future; to find ways of communication that lead to understanding; to acknowledge that the person being mentored is an individual; and the goal is growth, not cloning.

The stay in Britain enabled me to connect with British relatives. My Aunt Jean lived in a beautiful spot in the Scottish Highlands called Finzean. In fall 1981, I knew many relatives would be at Aunt Jean's for a family reunion on the same day I was scheduled to fly an F-111 low-level navigation mission to Scotland. Not two miles from Aunt Jean's house was an authorized practice low-level target. You can see where this one is going ... I decided it wouldn't be a big deal to stray a couple of miles off course and make a "visit" to the family reunion. I flew over the house at 100 feet and 700 miles per hour, not once but twice! The second pass was spectacular. My Aunt Jean and all the relatives were outside; she waved her dishtowel at me, and the rest were waving. I lit the afterburners and made an impressive departure into the vertical and over the horizon. I really thought I was "somebody"! Seemed like a good idea at the time.

Turns out Aunt Jean's neighbors didn't think so! The shock waves from the airplane had knocked down their flower gardens and the noise had terrified some villagers. Despite the fear and running for cover that was later described, someone did find time to break out a camera and get a picture of my second flyover.

I didn't know there was a problem until about a month later when the RAF low-fly division came to visit. I was confined to quarters for the month-long investigation and have never had a more miserable time. Being one who likes to focus on the positive, I will say I lost some weight and learned some lessons. As I stood at attention in front of Major General Baxter, the 3rd Air Force Commander, I didn't know what to expect. I knew the event had gone through the embassies and back to the United States. My Uncle Ralph from Milwaukee had called my parents in Iowa to ask if it was possible the

F-111 salute to his aunt costs pilot

MILDENHALL, England — An American pilot who repeatedly flew his F-111 plane over a Scottish town where his aunt lived has been disciplined by the Air Force, a 3rd Air Force spokesman said Monday.

About two months ago, Capt. Robert Vosburgh, 25, of the 20th Tac Fighter Wing, started buzzing the village of Finzean, the spokesman said.

'Broke the Rules'

"Basically, he broke the rules for low-altitude flying in the U.K.," said Capt. Stephen Manning. "That's why the Air Force took disciplinary action."

Vosburgh made low-level passes over his aunt's house while on routine training missions, Manning said. He added that pilots are bound to fly specific low-level routes, even on training missions.

Vosburgh was disciplined shortly before Christmas with reassignment to the United States, loss of a coveted assignment elsewhere in the Air Force and forfeiture of pay, Manning said.

No action against co-pilot

The F-111 is flown by two crew members, Manning said, but added that he did not know of any disciplinary action being taken against the co-pilot who flew with Vosburgh.

Vosburgh's aunt, Jean Williams, acknowledged her nephew's aerial greetings by waving outside her bungalow when the jet roared overhead, according to local English newspaper reports.

Manning said the Air Force has received other complaints about low-level flying, but "not all are justified."

Captain Bob he'd just heard about on the morning news could have been me. The British newspapers had a heyday.

I learned a great lesson from General Baxter. He shared with me the fact he had personally selected me as the only pilot in the 3rd Air Force to be in the first F-16 operational wing in Germany. As punishment for my air show antics, the F-16 assignment was cancelled. He asked me what assignment I thought appropriate. I took a stab and suggested an F-15 assignment might be the best thing for all parties. It would allow me to move on to that second operational aircraft I needed under my belt to apply to the test pilot school.

I hope he found some humor in this since the F-15 and F-16 were both outstanding fighter assignments, and it was audacious to suggest the F-15 as any kind of punishment. General Baxter did not act on my suggestion. I ended up going to the Fighter Lead-In Course in New Mexico as an instructor. Ultimately, I did get to fly the F-16 in Japan.

Now, back to the point. During our meeting, General Baxter suggested,

> *"As you go through life, make decisions as if I am standing next to you."*

Would I have done the air show over the family reunion if General Baxter were sitting in my F-111? I don't think so! I have followed this advice repeatedly through the years. Two lessons to be learned here: (1) If someone makes a mistake, give them the proper feedback and consequence, but also show hope for the future. (2) If you have tough decisions to make, without time for counsel, imagine your mentors standing alongside awaiting your most prudent move.

HALE BURR—CONSULTANT, FIGHTER PILOT AND RETIRED MAJOR GENERAL: *Mentoring is important to ensure that talented subordinates are rewarded and promoted (in a deliberate manner) to help the organization.*

However, there's a big difference between "mentors" and "sponsors." A mentor will identify the "best and brightest" to help them achieve their potential in the organization or institution. The mentor will teach, inspire and motivate those under him as they mature. A sponsor pushes his "good old boy" group or cronies who are probably sycophants who stroke his ego with the idea of benefiting themselves. This is detrimental to the organization in the long run.

PICTURE THEIR PRESENCE

BUZ BAXTER—BUSINESSMAN, FIGHTER PILOT AND RETIRED MAJOR GENERAL: *At age 3, I was selected to be the mascot of the local high school band directed by Cothburn O'Neal. We became life-long friends. It was my good fortune he became an inventor, U.S. Navy World War II fighter pilot, Ph.D., university professor, and author of a number of published novels. He was a man of huge intellect and could have sparred with anyone on almost any subject. For whatever reason he maintained a place for me under his wing. After his recent death, his widow told me Cothburn frequently called me the "son he never had"—perhaps my most treasured title.*

We had too little time to be together in person, or even on the telephone, but he was never far from my thoughts and prayers. When I faced a difficult situation I ordinarily prayed about it and spent some additional time asking myself: What would Cothburn do in this case? Frequently, I answered myself just by thinking of how carefully he looked at the facts, applied his values system, looked at alternatives, selected the best, bit the bullet and went to work. Just thinking I was doing it the way that

*would please him ordinarily put me on the right track. I
suppose I will always work to please Cothburn. Next to my
father, Cothburn O'Neal has impacted my life more than
anyone else I can think of. MORAL: For some decisions,
mentors are better equipped to lead you than your parents.*

Mentors can provide emerging leaders with content, confirmation and support. Throughout this book, I share the thoughts of more than a dozen leaders for whom I've worked, and from whom I've learned and adopted the great majority of my leadership values.

JOHN LORBER—VICE PRESIDENT, BOEING SPACE AND COMMUNICATIONS OPERATIONS AND RETIRED GENERAL: *Jim Allman was my Wing Commander at Upper Heyford, and he had a great technique. We were struggling a little bit, getting ready for an operational readiness inspection (ORI), and he sat everybody down after a practice exercise to go through, what he called, the "goods and bads." He would publicly acknowledge the goods, bring people up and slap them on the back. He never publicly acknowledged people associated with the bads, but we would discuss the events. That technique was extremely positive.*

Throughout my career, I've always felt the best job you have is the job you're doing right now. And if you're doing the job as well as you can possibly do it, that person who is overseeing you will likely become a mentor. He's going to say positive things about you and make certain your career is progressing for the good of you and the organization.

FIND A STYLE YOU CAN EMULATE

Pay close attention to the actions and styles of effective leaders. Effective leadership role models and mentors provide a great opportunity for us to observe and learn. Watch for the effect certain styles have on the team at all levels. Boil down the lessons to two or three salient points and test them in your leadership style. To improve your leadership skills you should look for effective leaders, observe their styles and then decide if those techniques work for you.

If you find a style you think is a match, take it, practice it and act it out. You've heard the suggestion that forcing yourself into a new behavior for just 30 days makes it a habit. I believe it!

MARK ANDERSON—CONSULTANT, FIGHTER PILOT AND RETIRED LIEUTENANT GENERAL: *I agree mentors are important, but in my experience, the true value is in the relationship between you and the mentor. I don't think you "seek" mentors. Rather, mentors become aware of you, and if the chemistry is right between you and the mentor, they will take the time to pass along experiences, advice, etc., that will prove valuable.*

One of the earliest counseling techniques I was shown is called the "sandwich" technique. The approach suggests we start with a positive, put the constructively critical feedback in the middle and finish with a positive. I wasn't very good at this the first time I tried it. I came off as too structured, insufficiently empathetic and self-serving. Nonetheless, I pursued this technique and, with time, have become much more comfortable with it. Leadership techniques need to be practiced.

If you don't have ready access to outstanding leadership or mentors, you might find direction in books. There are several management and leadership texts I recommend. I've taught from some of them and, from time to time, return to them for ideas.

Leadership is an Art by Max DePree
Nineteen Stars by Edgar Puryear
Taking Charge by Perry Smith

JEAN SCHLEMMER—CORPORATE EXECUTIVE: *James C. Collins has written two books,* Built to Last: Successful Habits of Visionary Companies *and* Good to Great: Why Some Companies Make the Leap . . . and Others Don't. *I'd given the second book,* Good to Great, *to my group because I wanted them to read about how a company goes from good to great. The opening line in the book is "Good is the enemy of great." So that was going to be the frame of reference. Collins' premise in the book is you start with somebody he calls a Level 5 leader; somebody for the most part who is the antithesis of a celebrity leader. They tend to be humble but driven. And then you get to the metaphor he uses, the bus. You've got to have the right people on the bus, the wrong people need to get off the bus and people need to be in the right seats.*

I suggest you partake in mentoring programs available in your profession and in contrasting industries as well. If none exist at your workplace, find a leader you respect and ask for counsel and support. I've yet to meet an outstanding leader who wasn't willing to provide feedback and counsel to emerging leaders who show potential and a willingness to be coached.

NEAL BARLOW—PROFESSOR, AIR FORCE PILOT AND COLONEL: *I've been fortunate over the years to work for some outstanding mentors. One of the things unique to the academy is that because we feel so strongly about mentors, every cadet commander is required to have a senior mentor. Cadet squadron commander, wing commander, group commander, soaring cadet commander and even a team captain has a mentor with whom they spend an hour a week. They discuss senior perspective to help them develop long-range vision and to handle the daily requirements of being a commander and a leader. I* *believe this approach and focus on mentorship has changed the cadet corps from one that learns by mistakes to one that learns to anticipate through mentorship. It has worked very well. I have had the opportunity in the last five years to mentor fifteen different cadet commanders.*

We spend a lot of time talking about the importance of setting high expectations, the importance of living those expectations and setting the example. Oftentimes you'll find young commanders who are very proud of putting out fires. Subordinates can come into the office with their problems and the leader can say, "Hey, I've got the solution. Let me take care if this for you." In reality, they aren't doing anybody any favors by not having the people underneath them find those solutions. We spend time talking to them about those sorts of issues, hoping they'll be better leaders sooner than later.

Many senior leaders talk about their superstar performers as individuals who are "coachable." They take opportunities to interact, solicit feedback and receive constructive criticism. If a senior leader sees change, improvement, enthusiasm and positive effect, they will continue to coach and add value to emerging leaders. You'll need to do some hard work. Take the feedback, turn it into action and modify it for specific situations and style. It makes more sense to learn from the sage advice of one who has already traveled the leadership path than to reinvent the process yourself.

I've been very fortunate to know several generous mentors. General Baxter has been there for me over the past twenty years, especially since his retirement from the Air Force in 1982. I've spent weekends with him where we went over the fundamentals of service, integrity, commitment and myriad other leadership qualities. He has also been available when I need situational advice. If you should be so lucky, you'll find the mentor relationship deeply rewarding, all the time increasing your effectiveness as a leader.

Three main points:
- Learn from outstanding leaders.
- Picture their presence.
- Find a style you can emulate.

BALANCE

Critical to our ability to lead and maintain the necessary stamina is proper balance. At times I've ignored the need for balance and found myself much less effective. If I don't get my exercise, I don't have the stamina to stay at the job for long periods of time. If I don't stay mentally stimulated, continuously improving myself, then I will not add the value I should as a leader. Finally, if I don't spend time with contrasting activities in order to maintain an emotional balance with family, friends and myself, I lose some of my perspective. I see three main areas that we have some control over:

- Physical,
- Mental, and
- Emotional balance.

Physical

Mental

Emotional

"He that would govern others,
first should be the master of himself."
Philip Massinger
1583–1640

PHYSICAL

"It is easier to maintain good health through proper exercise,
diet, and emotional balance than to regain it once it is lost."
Kenneth H. Cooper, M.D.

MARK ANDERSON—CONSULTANT, FIGHTER PILOT AND RETIRED LIEUTENANT GENERAL: *I aim for fifteen fitness events each month. When I ride the bike, go for a run, go to the fitness center, or go for a walk around the golf course, I record it on the calendar. It gives me the motivation to do it on a regular basis, and it has helped me maintain a regular regimen. I try to mix up the activities and keep the activity on a regular basis. It is my personal accountability for getting a variety of exercise, which is critical to my stamina.*

I recommend *The Aerobics Program for Total Well-Being,* by Dr. Kenneth Cooper. Since he is the expert, I'll simply quote from his book:

"The human body is just another part of the universe that is meant to be in perfect balance. We have been constructed in such a way that we need just so much exercise, no more and no less. We need just so much food of certain types. And we need just the right amount of sleep and relief from the tensions and stresses of daily life.

"If a person goes too far in either direction—too little or too much exercise, food or rest—then his or her entire physical and psychological system gets out of kilter. And where there is a lack of balance, there is also a lack of personal well-being.

"By the same token, on the positive side, where there is balance, there is a sense of well-being. And where there is perfect balance, there is what I call total well-being.

"Aerobic exercises refer to those activities that require oxygen for prolonged periods and place such demands on the body that it is required to improve its capacity to handle oxygen. As a result of aerobic exercise, there are beneficial changes that occur in the lungs, heart and vascular system. More specifically, regular exercise of this type enhances the ability of the body to move air into and out of the lungs, the total blood volume increases, and the blood becomes better equipped to transport oxygen.

"As with aerobic exercise, the fundamental principle that lies behind good eating habits is balance. If you find after reading this book that you need to lose some weight, you don't have to cut out every one of your favorite foods or go on some lopsided fad diet. Instead, we'll show you ways to keep a tasty balance in your daily menus even as you reduce the calories you consume.

"With the stresses and strains of modern life, increasing numbers of people are expressing a need to find the way to lasting inner peace, freedom from anxiety and solutions to other emotional problems. Everybody desperately wants to feel relaxed and happy about life, and to possess the extra reserves of energy that often accompany this sort of emotional equilibrium. But there is a constant tendency for minds and emotions under pressure to get out of balance—perhaps to swing like a psychological pendulum toward excessive concern for some personal problem, or to fall victim to unusual fatigue or lack of energy."

When I taught at the Air Force Academy, I was running twenty to thirty miles per week and have never felt better. I worked closer to a forty-hour week than ever before or since, leaving plenty of time for family and leisure. The Academy provided a one-hour lunch break for those who chose not to exercise; it was extended to two hours for those who would exercise. A group of four to six instructors would change into our running clothes and choose from a variety of courses. The fact we were exercising in the Rockies at 8,000 feet above sea level added to the aerobic conditioning. An added plus: the scenery was outstanding.

We'd typically run three to five miles, although when we trained for the Pike's Peak Marathon, we'd do longer weekend runs. My intention was never to win any of the many races we entered, but rather to finish them and derive as much stress-lowering benefit as possible. The longest I ever completed was the ten-mile Garden of the Gods race in Colorado Springs. Talk about slow! I did it in exactly 100 minutes, not ever expecting to set records or keep up with the leading runner. Unfortunately, just a few weeks before the Pike's Peak marathon, I broke my foot.

DAVID FISHER—BUSINESSMAN, FINANCIAL CONSULTANT AND ENTREPRENEUR: *"Excellence" in my opinion demands balance in your life. I see the major areas of my life as being connected—a husband, a father, a businessman, a citizen, a church member—so that what I do in one area ultimately has an affect on the others. Staying in proper physical shape is so fundamental to how we function in each area of our life. During times when my business demands are particularly heavy, I find it easier to slack off in exercising, and as a result it accentuates my feeling of tiredness. But you know, I really have no excuse. My family needs me to take proper physical care of myself—they need me to be around for a couple of more decades, not just a couple of more years.*

I left Colorado to fly the F-16 in Japan. As F-16 pilots we focused on anaerobic exercise and limited our aerobic exercise.

The F-16 was capable of sustaining 9 gs of acceleration (1 g is equivalent to the acceleration of gravity). For those inexperienced in high accelerations, let me take a shot at explaining the concept. Most of us are comfortable walking around at 1 g of acceleration. For the sake of example, I weigh somewhere around 200 pounds at 1 g of acceleration. My heart does just fine pumping blood up to my brain and to the rest of my body at this mass and acceleration (weight = mass × acceleration). Many of you have experienced more than 1 g on a roller coaster ride or in commercial airliners. If a commercial airliner, or any aircraft for that matter, is in level flight and 60 degrees of bank, its occupants experience 2 gs of acceleration. Next time you are in a commercial airliner, notice how your face sags and your weight increases in the turns.

If I am living at 2 gs, I now weigh around 400 pounds, and my heart has to work a bit harder to get the blood to my brain. Getting blood to the brain is somewhat critical to my operating normally! If the blood flow stops, or if the blood pressure drops too far, it is much like standing up too quickly from the couch. Have you ever noticed "stars" appearing in your peripheral vision when standing up too quickly? First we get tunnel vision, then we gray out, and then we pass out. If we do pass out, typically we don't remember it and, of course, are not functional.

In the F-16, at 9 gs, I weigh some 1800 pounds. My heart is

working very hard to keep me conscious, and if I am "too" aerobically fit with low blood pressure to start with, it makes the task of remaining conscious all the more difficult. So, we limited our running to no more than five miles per week and lifted weights for the sake of muscle tone and to help keep our blood pressure high enough to fight the physiological side of being a fighter pilot and the associated high accelerations.

There is an enormous difference in people's natural g-tolerance. Tall, lanky, long-distance runners are notorious for passing out at relatively low gs—four to six. Short, weight-lifting, smoking, drinking, wild-life, high-blood-pressure, always stressed-out folks tend to be great at resisting gs. Because their blood pressure is naturally high, they don't have to grunt and groan like the rest of us to resist the accelerations. I once saw a video of a short, muscular pilot singing the national anthem at 9 gs. He didn't have the distance (heart to brain) that the rest of us do and must have had incredibly high blood pressure. Personally I am fighting with all I have to remain conscious at those high accelerations. Takes all sorts.

DUTCH REMKES—FIGHTER PILOT AND AIR FORCE BRIGADIER GENERAL: *Push them away from their desks and toward the gym and track. Leading by personal example is critical here; make it well known that workout time is on your daily schedule, and it is not to be interrupted by business, unless there is an emergency.*

MENTAL

Mental balance to me is all about keeping perspective. It relates to many of the points you'll read in the portion of this chapter dedicated to emotional balance. It also relates to much of what you'll read in the section about having a positive attitude. I always like to take high-stress situations and put them into perspective. Usually, the seemingly significant issues won't matter a bit five years down the road—remind yourself of this. Also, it is only a job and life is far too short. I see many people lose their composure due to the stress associated with the workplace. First of all, it isn't healthy to walk around stressed out. Secondly, stress and the ensuing lack of focus typically detract from one's ability to calmly assess situations. In business this can lead to major errors in deal making, assessment of situations and handling of personnel issues. In the military this can lead to more serious consequences—some of which can be life threatening. Learn to compartmentalize and put issues into perspective—you'll be a better leader for it!

SAM WESTBROOK—CONSULTANT, BUSINESSMAN, FIGHTER PILOT AND RETIRED BRIGADIER GENERAL:
I like balance and stamina considered together, because I think having the one leads to the other. For most people, I think of balance in terms of four competing demands: Personal life, marriage or relationship, family life (adds children and relatives to marriage), and professional life. These four demand a lot more time than any of us have to give, so we have to find an appropriate balance. Most younger people throw every ounce of energy at professional life and give what is left over to the other three. Then it starts to go awry—divorce, alcohol, drugs and depression. The hard part is how to recognize when the balance is right. There is no right answer, but my personal choice is to try and feel equally guilty about what I am not doing for each of the four. When things are roughly in balance, I find my stamina is there—I have a zest for life that is like rocket fuel. I may work fewer hours from a professional standpoint, but I am very productive and am happy to get back to work most Mondays.

When I was younger I was very driven and found myself attempting to juggle too many balls. I wanted to do everything perfectly and found myself terribly diluted. Looking back I feel I would have been more effective had I limited my focus to a few important areas, taken vacations, and better balanced my life.

EMOTIONAL

JOHN FARRISH—CORPORATE EXECUTIVE: *I start my days with a reminder of three things I've found make a difference in the way I approach the day and balance my tasks: Grace, Acceptance and Living in the Present.*

From the first time I heard John's thoughts, I've found many opportunities to call upon his simple reminder. I'll do my best to share his explanation of all three areas and suggest we call this the "GAP" approach to balance.

JOHN FARRISH—CORPORATE EXECUTIVE: *Over a decade ago I was in Denver doing interviews. While a lot of things externally in my life were working ... I became aware my life wasn't working well. It was something I'd never felt before, and I didn't know what it was—just that it wasn't the job, and it wasn't family. That day I started on a journey to resolve the issues and find a better balance. There is a book called* Care of the Soul *by Thomas Moore. He wrote that life is difficult, and it is important we take care of our souls. I did a lot of reading on Eastern religions, Western religions and different philosophies. Through a two-year journey and plenty of workshops where I looked for a reason I didn't feel inner peace, three things were consistent in all of my research. Grace, Acceptance and Living in the Present. These are three things I never actually achieve—this is a journey, although I think about them eight to ten times each day. They help me do a reality check.*

The last of those, living in the present, mindfulness or flow can manifest itself in physical activities. I remember when I used to swim a lot and when it got to the point where it was effortless, it just seemed to happen. Times when I come to work and it is quiet, I become tremendously productive. The similarities between those times in my life when it works are that I'm living completely in the present. The more I can operate from that point of view and get into a state of flow, the more effective my life is.

I take John's thoughts on living in the present to a practical level each and every day. Many of us have grown up utilizing the Day Timer, Franklin or Covey systems. What I've learned is these systems are very helpful so long as we get to the point where we are actually doing something!

I do believe we all need to have dreams and long-term goals. However, it is what we do today and how we do it that will either hurt or help us in attaining those goals.

"I tell you the past is a bucket of ashes."
Carl Sandburg, 1878–1967

It is very tempting to hammer out vision statements and spend time planning for the future. It is also quite easy to spend a lot of time reflecting on what we've done in the past. Both the past and the future need to be considered if we want to learn from history and attach ourselves to worthy goals. Strategic planning and defining our vision is also critical in defining a path; however, it is what we do today, right now, that actually moves us down a path.

DAVID FISHER—BUSINESSMAN, FINANCIAL CONSULTANT AND ENTREPRENEUR: *It has been my experience that even in the very best of times, I feel a longing for something more. That something is spiritual, and I think that addressing the spiritual need is fundamen-*

tal to meeting the emotional need. When our spiritual search has real answers, our lives have a purpose that transcends our careers and even our families, and it brings great emotional balance.

During my tenure in a start-up business, I spent a lot of time focusing on vision and strategy. Some of my partners were into reinventing the business plan on what seemed like a daily basis. One firm (which I ultimately took over as CEO) hired strategic planners and talked far too much about the seemingly infinite opportunities. Small businesses, particularly start-up businesses, need to find their vision, define their strategy and then get on with the execution.

> *"There is no more fatal blunder than he who consumes the greater part of his life getting his living."*
> ### Henry David Thoreau,
> ### *1817–1862*

Something that really helps me balance complex situations is to not linger in the decision–making process. Early in my military training we were introduced to a concept called "command decision." The point of the training was that ultimately someone has to make a decision so we can move forward. The "buck" has to stop somewhere!

Personally, I have not found a more frustrating environment than one where decisions are not made in a timely fashion. I like to use an analogy where we're jogging down a path, come to a Y, and must decide whether to go right or left. Although, in hindsight, we may find going right is better than left, or vice versa, we need to take the available facts, decide on which route appears best from a logical and emotional basis, and keep on running. I can promise you if we don't make decisions, and if we don't create a forward momentum, it is very unlikely we'll ever succeed. Make a decision, commit to it, lead your team with confidence and do it right now—live in the present.

I have an example of poor decision-making my wife Cindy experienced firsthand. It shows how important it is to make a decision and stick with it. In 1979, I was training to fly the F-111 in Mountain Home, Idaho. Cindy was finishing college in Texas and had come to Idaho to visit for a weekend. She was fortunate to hitch a ride on her father's corporate airplane for the trip back to Texas. The plane, a Piper Navajo, is a twin-engine business airplane that seats six or seven people. The inexperienced pilot and Cindy were flying over Albuquerque at night when the pilot decided to continue on to Fort Worth without a previously planned fuel stop (mistake number one).

As they flew, the radar picked up a line of thunderstorms in front of Fort Worth. The pilot decided to try to go around them (mistake number two). As most experienced pilots have learned, you don't out climb or outrun many thunderstorms. It became apparent they weren't going to make it around the storms, so he decided to land at the nearest airfield and refuel (a good decision). Have you spent much time in eastern New Mexico? Not much there, especially in the way of airfields.

Eventually they found one and prepared to land. Approaching the runway, the pilot was flying too quickly (mistake number three), but pulled the power to idle to land. After touching down, he decided they wouldn't be able to stop in the available runway and pushed the throttles up to full power to takeoff (mistake number four). Since they were low on fuel and the runway was so short, he next decided they wouldn't be able to take off in the remaining runway. So, he pulled the power back to idle and slammed on the brakes (a good decision just in the nick of time).

The deceleration caused fuel to vent on the exhaust manifolds and started the engines on fire. Picture this remote airfield in New Mexico, at night, with the airplane decelerating down the runway, both engines on fire, and eventually stopping just beyond the end of the runway. I'm sure you'll agree the decision-making process was less than optimum (particularly since my wife was on board!).

As it turned out, there was significant damage to one of the engines. Cindy called me after she calmed her nerves. She shared that she hadn't really understood how to open the door of the Piper Navajo when it was first described to her. However, when the burning airplane stopped, she found a way to get out and away posthaste!

The next day, the pilot suggested they take off, with just one engine working, and fly the remaining distance to Fort Worth (mistake number six). The charter group for whom he had worked fired him that day. Cindy returned to Fort Worth on a bus! For years I had a quote hanging in my office that is appropriate here:

"If you find yourself in a hole, quit digging."
Author Unknown

I want to emphasize a decision made now may turn out to be the wrong decision. That's okay! Be certain to admit to the fact as soon as possible, make appropriate modifications, and move on. Continuous experimentation with ideas is what gets a business moving forward with a momentum that allows some failures along the way, but ultimately it gets us out there where the great ideas can evolve.

JOHN FARRISH—CORPORATE EXECUTIVE: *Acceptance is based upon the truth that I can't control the world, and I can't control other people. People are going to be what they are, and the world is going to evolve the way it is going to evolve. What I need to do is realize those things I cannot change. It doesn't mean I don't want to be proactive about changing and improving my life, but it really wastes a lot of energy, like pushing on a string, if I work on changing those things I can't.*

As our head of the investment sales group at Norwest, John Farrish asked we not hire anybody who had changed jobs more than three times in the previous five years. Why? Because we need to accept people for what they are and realize they'll very likely change jobs another three times in the next five years. We want people that stick to the job, long term, and add value to us for many years to come.

Some people think it is natural to be constantly on the prowl for new employment opportunities. The exuberance of the '90s reinforced this for many disciplines, including technology, where supply was low and demand high. Many, many people moved from job to job, each time getting a boost in pay and adding less value than they could have longer term at any one of those jobs.

If you think you can change repeat offenders you are wasting your time. Time and time again I see this in my businesses. Find people who consistently stay in employment positions, make a contribution and become long-term team members.

I once met a marketing person who presented herself by giving a résumé that included work at half a dozen prominent firms. She went on and on about all of the different experiences she'd had along the way. When I took over that company, she was one of the first to go, by her choice. She had shown no endurance, no commitment to a strategy, and no loyalty to the people who hired her. I don't know that she ever made a significant contribution or followed through on any of the marketing projects she started. She created a flurry of mindless activities, new charts, hired third-party consultants and went to social events and cocktail parties to talk about her position (and so on).

People like this are able to live in the environment created by a large organization much more easily than in a start-up where everyone has to carry their load. In either case, the leader needs to deal with this sort of behavior aggressively and help the offender on to the next charade. Many have been able to ratchet themselves up in compensation and position by moving so quickly they are never held accountable. Don't expect to change these folks. Do everything you can to avoid hiring them. It is more effort to get rid of the bad eggs than to hire the good ones up front. Take the additional time from the first to find the right person.

Treating people with grace entails creating a positive environment. I've never seen any benefit from being rude or critical, especially in public. No matter what the situation, no matter how upset you may be, it is better to be pleasant (while honest) with team members.

It is disappointing how infrequently we are kind to those around us. It is also clear how large the opportunity is for us to benefit from being kind, flattering, positive and encouraging.

JOHN FARRISH—CORPORATE EXECUTIVE: *Grace has always been tougher to get my arms around. One of the great examples of grace was when, the day after President Kennedy was shot, Jackie Kennedy wrote a letter to Lyndon Johnson. Her letter captured the spirit of what he must be going through moving into his new job. It was an incredible example of grace and how one should live their life. I find the more I'm able to be better at living in the present, acceptance and grace, the more my professional and personal life works.*

John and I used to travel together, and he taught me many lessons about interacting with others. Take, for example, the airport check-in agent. These people deal with upset customers all day long, with requests for upgrades, changes due to weather, changes due to strikes, and customers from all over the United States and the world. John and I would get the same economy class tickets for these flights, yet he seemed to get upgrades to first class on a routine basis. I decided to watch. He was incredibly pleasant to the airline representative. John would say, "Good morning, how's your day going?" The gate agent would reply, "Fine . . . Mr. Farrish." John would ask, "What a lovely name, how do you pronounce it?" The gate agent would reply, "Mayaguez, Mr. Farrish. Here's your seat, 1A, and have a great day." Take the time, listen to people, find their pain, make their day, and you will be rewarded many times over.

I travel to Chicago on a frequent basis and have made it my intent to say something pleasant to the gate agents every single time. They now are getting to know me, and my life is less stressful because of their ability to streamline my check-in and seating assignment. Recently, I had several of my team traveling with me, and we were all upgraded to first class. Just because! What goes around comes around—never forget.

DR. SANDRA DAVIS—CORPORATE EXECUTIVE, AUTHOR AND PSYCHOLOGIST: *What people need is to have enough resilience in themselves that they can be centered to weather any storm. That's an easy thing to say. How do you do that? I don't think it is just about balance. I think it's about all the passions we have in our lives, and I think it's about making sure we take time for those things that really matter and are at the heart of our existence. That means you find a way to pursue your passions in whatever way possible. I don't think it's about dividing your calendar up into "Well, I did my one hour for family today, and I did my one hour for this other passion I have, and my one hour for that." I think it's about pursuing things that are really important to you as a human being. For me, it's spending time with family, with friends, and having time to learn. I think for me learning is a real passion. So today I am learning Chinese and maybe next time I decide I'm going to learn to fly. It's following some passion I have for myself.*

There is a spirituality and values component for which

you need to take time in your life. Remember your "work" is both paid and nonpaid. The person who's in a leadership role, not only "works" for their organization, they may also "work" nonpaid roles in the community.

People have the most trouble when they don't know who they are at their core. Steve Covey starts with "First know yourself." I think that's great advice. I think you need to understand what you do well and what you do poorly. In those times when you feel really alone in some decision, you can bring people around who fill in the gaps for you. And you have to be strong enough to say I need other people to come fill the gaps. It's a paradox.

A lot about leadership is a paradox. You have to be strong enough to know you need help. You have to be strong enough to stand alone and yet be willing to ask other people for input and to draw upon them. But if you aren't centered about who you are, what you believe in, and why you're doing what you're doing, you won't have the strength to be vulnerable.

In this chapter we've spoken of balance. Balance leads to higher levels of endurance and a more enjoyable life. Remember three things:

- Stay fit, get aerobic exercise and be prepared to accelerate and pull some gs!
- Keep a mental balance by prioritizing and scheduling time for yourself, your work, your significant other and your family.
- Find an emotional balance that works for you. It may be through a close set of friends, your religion, or a set of values that helps you look in the mirror and plan your day (Grace, Acceptance, and Living in the Present).

TEAM

In this section, focused on team, we'll look at:
- Clarity,
- Hiring, Firing and Empowerment, and
- Ensuring Accountability.

4

CLARITY

Everyone on your team must have a clear understanding of your vision. It doesn't do much for you until it is communicated throughout the entire organization—many times and in as many formats as appropriate to get everyone's attention. Even if you think you are sufficiently communicating the vision, you probably aren't. Some change management guidelines suggest you need to communicate five-fold what feels right. So, in this chapter I discuss:

- Everyone must understand the vision.
- Annual reinvention exercises.
- Effective communication.

"In the long run, men hit only what they aim at."
Henry David Thoreau,
1817–1862

Understand the Vision

Reinvention Exercises

Effective Communication

EVERYONE UNDERSTANDING THE VISION

I've observed some very effective CEOs and noted they repeat the corporate story over and over again. If you read *Jack: Straight from the Gut* by Jack Welch, you'll note he spent an enormous amount of time getting the word out to the field. It is a monumental task, often frustrating and sometimes seemingly insurmountable, and it takes your concentration and endurance to get the job done. Even then, it may not be realistic to expect the entire team to listen to and remember the company vision. The larger the organization, the more likely you won't get the word all the way to the last employee. The question is, How do you get as many employees as possible to care enough to study the vision, understand its implications and relate it to their daily activities?

JEAN SCHLEMMER—CORPORATE EXECUTIVE: *How you get the culture communicated throughout the company requires work. I thought we were doing a good job of communicating among ourselves in my group. And I discovered I was making some assumptions (shame on me) that what was communicated in our group was getting communicated down. Now some of the "information" got communicated, but culture, style, the style of the group and the style of the company didn't get communicated. What got communicated was the personal style of the individual business unit leader.*

MARK ANDERSON—CONSULTANT, FIGHTER PILOT AND RETIRED LIEUTENANT GENERAL: *It doesn't matter a whole lot what you call it (vision, mission, goals, strategy), the important point is that members of the organization know and understand what you're about, where you're going, and how you plan to get there. And you can't overcommunicate. Important points must be* *repeated multiple times in many forms for them to be understood and remembered.*

My personal goal is that everyone in the company be able to give the "elevator talk" (share our company vision) during the course of an elevator ride. A three-bullet-point version is ideal for this endeavor. I'm not talking about an elevator ride in the Sears tower!

JOHN LORBER—VICE PRESIDENT, BOEING SPACE AND COMMUNICATIONS OPERATIONS AND RETIRED GENERAL: *I tell people I'm going to give them a vision that's on a heading of somewhere between 330 and 030 degrees (referring to a compass heading). I'm not going to say it's 359. Because I might be wrong or I might be off a little bit. And if I say it's a hard heading of 359, that's where we're going to go to and nobody will want to deviate from the heading. I want to see some creativity in my team. You need to keep them focused on going in a general direction. I like to think of that direction as a sector of about 60 degrees.*

Don't make your story too complicated. Dilution and the resultant lack of focus on the critical tasks at hand can have a major negative effect on your team. If the leader hasn't made their goals clear, especially the three primary goals, members of the organization will not have a clear picture where they should align, how they should support and where they should put their efforts. Figure out how many "brain bytes" you have to spend; select only enough tasks that can be done in an exemplary manner and then adjust with the times. I'll suggest you'll have some people who, when given a complicated vision, will fit the description "8k in a 64k environment" (as in computer random access memory). Keep it simple.

SAM WESTBROOK—CONSULTANT, BUSINESSMAN, FIGHTER PILOT AND RETIRED BRIGADIER GENERAL: *A word of caution here. I have been in organizations that set "stretch" goals so unrealistic they were a tremendous downer. If you are going to set stretch goals, make sure you have a good communication package to go along with them so people understand why you think they could happen.*

I've mentioned before that I strive to take people and get above-average results. One way to do this is by making it very clear that I expect everyone, from the receptionist on up, to be aware of what we are all about as a team and where we are heading.

ROGER SCHMITT—BUSINESSMAN, FIGHTER PILOT AND RETIRED COLONEL: *Ineffective strategic planning has led to the demise of many otherwise healthy organizations. Vision must be leader-initiated, positive and inspiring, shared and supported, detailed and comprehensive. It must, at the minimum, answer the questions: Why does the organization exist? Who does it serve? and What are the organization's primary services and products?*

In many organizations, a significant proportion of the workforce simply puts in their time with no plan or goals. I admit there have been times when I've envied those who can go to work at 9 A.M. and leave at 5 P.M., never taking any of the worries home or feeling any accountability for the company's success or failure.

JOHN LORBER—VICE PRESIDENT, BOEING SPACE AND COMMUNICATIONS OPERATIONS AND RETIRED GENERAL: *I had a young guy who ran our base recreation center at Kunsan, Korea. I was the Commander of the Pacific Air Force at the time when I came to visit the base. As I walked into the fitness center, I saw a list hanging on the wall outlining what he was going to do to improve the recreation center with all the details, including a timeline. There were some aggressive goals. I asked him, "How do you intend to achieve this? You don't have the money to do some of the things you're asking." He said, "That's why I'm showing it to you, General."*

I looked at the things he had done in the past with a very limited budget and realized how much he had accomplished to date. Well, he got the money because he put his vision out there for everyone to see. He moved forward with a commitment and optimism that convinced me he'd get the job done and improve the facilities. He did more in one year to improve the facility than anybody had in the prior ten years. And when it got to the end of his one-year tour, he had a first-rate facility where everybody enjoyed coming to work out. He improved the likelihood of his accomplishing his vision by (1) Making his strategy clear and hanging it for everyone to see and, (2) Having the courage and confidence to ask for support.

ANNUAL REINVENTION EXERCISES

I rely upon a Vision, Strategy, Tactics and Commitment program. My teams do an annual reinvention exercise, which leads to refinement of the company vision. When complete, we come up with a strategy to divide and conquer the tasks at hand. We assign specific accountability and ask for a commitment from all players to attack their tasks with a vengeance. Every year, involving every person! (To ensure we remain on-task during the exercise, we limit it to one hour per week for a three-month period.)

JEAN SCHLEMMER—CORPORATE EXECUTIVE: *What I've learned in the past year is you can give people a little too much freedom. There are such things as best practices, corporate consistency and other components needed to run a larger company. I think it is worth going through the exercise for everyone to realize that. I think people believed they had a great deal of freedom to experiment. I've used the word "experiment" a lot, and some people get scared by the word because it sounds scientific—and there can be failure in there. In* Built to Last: Successful Habits of Visionary Companies, *James C. Collins talks about trying a whole bunch of new ideas. Keep what works, throw out what doesn't work and then relate it to the "often delighted, never satisfied" concept.*

A brokerage sales force I once managed was a typical "come to work and see what happens" group. Some of the sales people had been in their jobs for more than a decade and had a book of business that was providing a decent income, but they lacked the focus and drive needed to take the business to a higher level.

Rolling into that job, I had a plan to start by observing the personnel and their behaviors. Ultimately, I ended up eliminating some of the top sales producers. It wasn't a problem of individual production but the negative effect they had on the team. More than 80 percent of the team was unable to add full value because of the manipulation and inefficiencies of its top producers. I called this "holding the office hostage" and quickly put an end to the arrangement where the team's efforts were aligned to make a few people very successful. Instead, we built an environment where everyone contributed to the overall team vision. There was quite a bit of resistance from my bosses to getting rid of the producers who were responsible for more than 50 percent of the office's total gross revenue. However, we recovered to the same productivity level within two months and surpassed revenue expectations from that year forward. The team was told that those producers had decided to pursue other opportunities and were asked to rally and fill the void.

Once the team was cleaned up and opportunities were there for the entire group, we embarked on an exercise that took three months each year. (Again, in no more than one-hour weekly increments.) The first month included a presentation by me and action by the team members to define our *Vision*. We followed with a *Strategy* exercise and, finally, a *Tactics and Commitment* exercise. By the time we reached and completed Tactics, we had specific, daily, tasks that moved the team in a coordinated fashion towards a common vision in which they had ownership. In the past, I've put those daily tactics on a plaque on team members' desks and encouraged the use of computer-based programs that include recurring tasks and daily reminders. I also conducted a monthly, written rollup of events to the entire team about individual progress as an effective accountability tool.

I've used this outline over the past decade to help teams achieve clarity in vision. There are any number of ways this can be improved, dissected and criticized, but I'll tell you this much: If you do it, if you follow through, if you take the initiative to walk your team through the exercise, you WILL make a difference.

JIM PASCHALL—RANCHER, BUSINESSMAN, FIGHTER PILOT AND RETIRED LIEUTENANT COLONEL: *Like a good politician, always have a few main points that can be followed without a lot of brainwork. Not everyone in the area needs to know all the details.*

First, some definitions:

Vision—defines our desired future.

Strategies—broad plans of action to fulfill mission and achieve vision.

Tactics—specific and detailed actions to achieve goals. Who, what, where, when, how and why.

The opening slide for the Vision exercise includes quotes from a June 1999 *Wall Street Journal* article quoting Mr. Jerry Porras, professor of organizational behavior at Stanford.

"Many organizations devote too much time developing mission statements and not enough time meeting them . . . still, experts contend that companies can benefit from a vision if it is implemented the right way. One study shows that 18 'visionary' companies outperformed a control group in the stock market by more than six to one, measured over the period 1926 to 1990. Jerry Porras, professor of organizational behavior at Stanford and the study's co-author, says 'visionary' companies stand out partly by setting ambitious goals, communicating them to employees and following what he terms a 'core ideology'—a purpose beyond making money. For instance, he cites Walt Disney Company's aim of 'making people happy' as critical to its success.

"'You can sit down and generate a vision in a few days, but that isn't enough,' Porras says. 'You need to align the organization to achieve it. Organizations must also change their missions and visions to keep up with the times.'"

I take the team through an exercise that involves envisioning utopia as it relates not only to the business and professional lives, but to personal lives as well. We all know if team members don't have their personal lives squared away, it is unlikely they'll be performing at an exemplary level in their jobs. I've also found it helpful to give specific examples of vision—"vision scraps," from previous exercises. By putting those in the presentation it gives people a feel for where they can and should go with their thoughts. Examples from an institutional brokerage office:

"My vision for 2005 is to establish myself as a quality sales representative with approximately 1,000 clients. My clients will be a diverse group of banks, corporations and thrifts. Service and integrity will be an intricate part of my vision."

"My 2005 vision includes building a trusting relationship with the team, finding ways to be of continued support for the people I work for and finding ways to further educate myself in the business."

"My vision plan for 2005 includes being the top producer in the Omaha sales office with production of $1,000,000. This will allow me to do the things I want for the personal, professional, married and family components of my life. We'll start our hunt for the cabin in Colorado we always wanted and start looking at colleges for our son."

"My vision for 2005 is to do everything I can to enable whomever I may assist to accomplish their goals, and thereby contribute to the bottom line of our office production."

Other excerpts from vision statements:
- Build leadership/management skills
- Improve my professional image
- Increase my value to the team
- Increase my personal income
- Be viewed as a person of utmost integrity and character
- Retire at age 55
- Maintain and expand my customer base
- Solidify commercial banking relationships
- Become a mortgage-backed security expert
- Become more aggressive and proactive
- Have fun at work
- Continue my self-education
- Pass my securities license examination
- Better support the people I work for

- Find a balance between work and home
- Take a full week of vacation to a foreign country
- Lead a team expanding into a new area
- Start a family
- Buy a newer (not new, just newer) car

From these discussions the team members go off and work on their personal visions. During the month, I spend time with all team members and assist them in working through the exercise.

The second month we talk about a strategy to reach the vision. We decide which battles we're going to fight. I like to start this session with a reminder that we're looking for the right balance, the right goals and the right approach as a team. I like to share some philosophical banter to keep the team in the right frame of mind. H. Jackson Brown wrote a book called *Life's Little Instruction Book*, from which I share:

- Stop blaming others. Take responsibility for every area of your life.
- Don't waste time learning the "tricks of the trade." Instead, learn the trade.
- Demand excellence and be willing to pay for it.
- Think big thoughts, but relish small pleasures.
- Never deprive someone of hope; it might be all they have.
- Take time to smell the roses.
- Strive for excellence, not perfection.
- Keep your desk and work area neat.
- Be punctual and insist on it in others.
- Don't waste time responding to your critics.
- Never give up on what you really want to do. The person with big dreams is more powerful than one with all the facts.
- Wear out, don't rust out.

Also, from *Creating Excellence: Managing Corporate Culture, Strategy and Change in the New Age* by Michael A. Silva, Craig R. Hickman:

"Today, finite resources, new technology, and accelerating change are placing unprecedented pressure on every organization. Only those . . . who learn to anticipate and even invent the future will profit from, rather than be surprised by, change."

It is also important to point out we very likely won't complete our strategy as originally designed because of unanticipated, autonomous forces. We need to be flexible. However, we will most certainly never execute our strategy nor even get close to it if we don't at least aim at a target.

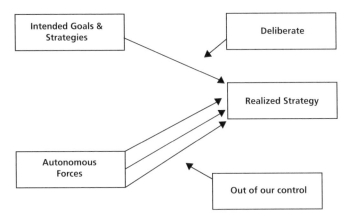

I lived through one company's well-intentioned plans for entering the online brokerage marketplace. The numbers, in the late '90s, were positively compelling. The migration from the more expensive full-service brokerage marketplace to the online brokerage solution was impressive. At one time, the market valuations per customer were in excess of $10,000. Online brokerage companies were spending some $400 in acquisition costs per customer and seeing company valuations at up to 25 times their acquisition cost. Seemed like a compelling business plan at the time. The vision and strategy were supported by real data, and the team was motivated to make it work, hoping to improve upon earlier models by learning from the mistakes and inefficiencies of predecessors.

However, the autonomous forces came in and knocked the wind out of the strategy. The securities markets took a dive, online valuations dropped by more than 90 percent, and customers shied away from online trading. The best of plans sometimes become ineffective because of changing environments.

In this particular example, the process of constant reinvention refocused the company to online 401(k) retirement programs, a market emerging just as the online brokerage markets were submerging. The move allowed the company to utilize its strengths in brokerage and investments, as well as in clearing and information technology.

DUTCH REMKES, FIGHTER PILOT AND AIR FORCE BRIGADIER GENERAL: *If the priorities change, stop all work and make sure everyone knows what the new priorities are. You don't want to waste even one minute of energy on an old priority.*

Back to the process! In the third month of the annual exercise, I put tactics and commitment together. It seems to be human nature not to follow through, even after significant effort has been expended in coming up with a strategy to define personal and team vision. I've watched some large organizations run people through extensive training and offsite exercises to come up with vision and mission statements. I've then seen those employees return to "business as usual," with the overall effort to execute the new vision put on the back burner.

It is critical that we EXECUTE. We must drive to specific goals with commitment and accountability on a daily basis. To get your team to function at a high productivity level you need to ensure it has a game plan each and every day. Some of my top-producing sales people used to know the amount of production they had to meet on an hourly basis to hit their annual plan. They knew they had to sell over $1,000 per hour and that their taking a long lunch, or not getting around to the toughest part of the job—actually making the calls and selling the product—would bring them in short of their vision. It boils down to activity supporting the strategy.

DAVID FISHER—BUSINESSMAN, FINANCIAL CONSULTANT AND ENTREPRENEUR: *Employees respond to a vision cast with enthusiasm by the whole of management. The best example I can think of is GE, when Jack Welch clearly stated GE would be in the top three companies of any business they were in, or they would exit the business. A clear, unmistakable vision—it did wonders for GE.*

So, how do you get down to the actual tactics? This simple example relates to numbers—a sales representative with multiple product lines.

Shawn, an investment salesperson, said his vision was to do $1 million in gross revenue production for the year in question. His strategy, based on his customer makeup, was to achieve 50 percent of the production by selling government treasury securities, 25 percent via municipal bonds, and 25 percent via money market deposits. Let's focus on Shawn's money market business.

Shawn's revenues from money market deposits were derived from a payment of 0.5 percent he received for the balances on hand. Shawn had a good start on the money market deposits but needed to bring the balances up from $75 million to $125 million over the next year to reach his goals. He needed to add just over $400,000 per month in net new deposits. That worked out to about $100,000 per week. His institutional customers had average money market deposits of $50,000, so he had to add two new institutional money market customers per week. History showed he had to make twenty-five cold prospecting calls for every new customer. He therefore needed to make fifty prospect calls per week, or ten per day.

Shawn held himself accountable by having that task on his daily calendar and making it a high priority. Every morning he came in and made the ten required calls. At the end of the year he had exceeded his goal, his closure rate from those phone calls having increased with practice. In the brokerage business it is a game of activity and numbers. There is no magic to the game, simply a need for discipline to reach the number of activities necessary for a certain production level. Daily accountability is a must.

I like to take my sales people through this exercise every year, right down to the daily activity level. Try it; you'll like it.

RANDY MEHLIN—AIRLINE PILOT, FIGHTER PILOT AND RETIRED LIEUTENANT COLONEL: *Clear-cut, definable, measurable, and challenging goals . . . every book you've ever read says the same thing. If you don't know where you're going, how will you know when you get there? There are things besides corporate goals that are worth considering. Maybe we can look at individual goals (education, quality of life) or community charitable efforts (time and money), school involvement, or environmental goals instead of making more widgets at a lower unit cost. Solicit input so folks feel they have a stake in the accomplishment of the goals. You will probably get more ideas and more people to feel they are making progress towards a goal that's personally satisfying or important.*

We often overlooked periodically evaluating where we stand. I like doing little projects around the farm on my days off, like building a fence. There you can step back, put you hands on your hips and see you've actually accomplished something. With a lot of jobs or tasks it's not so easy. You get into a dull monotonous routine of going to work day after day and feeling all you did was put in your time. Make an effort to show team members where we stand. Often a lot of important things accomplished get lost in the daily grind . . . we can't see the forest for all the trees!

EFFECTIVE COMMUNICATION

First of all, everyone works for someone. The CEO works for the board of directors, the entire company works for the customers, the senior staff works for the CEO, the colonels work for the generals, and so on. If all of the aforementioned parties communicate effectively, team goals are much more likely to be reached.

By treating people with the grace discussed in the earlier chapter on balance and stamina, you'll be much more effective. Any interactions we have should include a caring attitude and sincere concern for the well-being of the participants. Whether we are giving an annual review, a monthly one-on-one, or a written warning, it will be more effective if we can surround any bad news with a positive spin— the sandwich approach.

An example: "Good morning, Jim. I'm glad we could spend some time together. I'd like to start by saying we consider you a valuable member of the team. Your productivity ranks in the top 10 percent of all our sales people. I've got an idea and would like to offer my help in moving you to even higher levels of productivity. It came to my attention you were abrasive with one of your teammates, and although I'm not interested in those details, I would like to suggest that if you want to provide feedback to Susan, you do it in a more positive manner. Susan is a valuable team member and critical to your success. I think you'll want to keep her motivated and willing to help you meet your goals. Here are some techniques I use for providing similar feedback . . . Lastly, I want to reiterate my belief that you are a valuable team member. My hope is that with an atmosphere including continuous improvement and open feedback, we can make your contribution even more significant. I'd like you to work on your communication techniques with other employees and see if you can improve your productivity beyond the already impressive levels I see today. "

As a leader, it is critical you schedule regular one-on-one meetings with your direct reports. In a small company, I suggest these sessions should extend into the company ranks as far as your schedule allows. You'll learn so much more about what is going on in the company if you can find time for "two-down" interviews with the reports of your reports. It shows these employees you care and gives you the opportunity to see how your management team is doing in the eyes of their direct reports. I make it a point to write down suggestions and questions that come from these meetings and provide feedback to the individual. Follow through and show you are genuine. It builds loyalty from your team.

RANDY MEHLIN—AIRLINE PILOT, FIGHTER PILOT AND RETIRED LIEUTENANT COLONEL: *Be a "B.S. Screen." You don't need to pass everything down the chain. I used to dislike commanders who would come back from daily meetings with notes and read them to the entire group. Some things are not applicable. You decrease the effectiveness of the group by sharing all tasks and problems with all people. Be a filter, set priorities and share the relevant information.*

Conflicts will happen, personalities will differ, and misinformation and rumors will surface in any organization. If you think back on all of the conflicts you've been asked to resolve, all of the feedback you've received that was erroneous, and all of the wasted time sorting out differences, you'll agree most of those issues could have been resolved if the involved parties had simply met face-to-face and talked through the details.

If a team member comes to me and relates a problem concerning another team member, in almost every case, I ask that the other team member come to my office so that we talk this out. After the issue has been discussed I suggest that in the future, the two sit down and resolve their issues without my involvement. It seems to be natural for team members to go to their supervisor to complain about other team members. DO NOT ALLOW THIS! If they have a problem, they should discuss it with the other party. The exception, of course, is when the complaint is legal or work-environment related.

My teams hear about the "Sundown Rule." If anyone has a conflict, a perceived difference, has heard a rumor about someone, or needs further information to resolve an issue, I suggest they go face-to-face with the person before the end of the workday. We don't want people carrying issues home, fretting about conflicts or being distracted from their daily tasks. My experience shows 95 percent of the issues that distract, hurt feelings or cause conflict are miscommunication. Almost every time two people sit down and do the "he said, she said" exercise, it turns out issues were miscommunicated, exaggerated or simply untrue. I can't count the number of times two people have looked at each other and said, "I'm really glad we sat down and talked this out. I thought you were upset about A, B and C, and it turns out someone misunderstood." Force the situation, make people communicate directly if there is an issue and have them do it before sundown.

Another way to reduce conflict is to align compensation incentives so individuals or groups need to work together for common goals. Healthy competition can be productive. However, if two groups within the same organization have the same target market with competing product lines, or there isn't sufficient clarity in the vision and strategy to clearly separate responsibilities, there can be problems. I've taken two sales groups challenged with going after the same market with two different approaches and combined their structures. No matter which approach landed the customer, everyone was compensated. If you think about it, this leads to the group taking the most effective course for customer acquisition because of a common goal. It gets rid of the "we versus they" complications and increases the overall productivity and effectiveness of the team.

I once read a book, a very long book, about how to communicate a change or an innovation. It went into great detail about how the new idea needs to be disseminated amongst all interested parties. The bottom line of the book was that we don't communicate very well and need to go well beyond what feels natural.

I mentioned earlier that even if you feel you are communicating well, up it five-fold.

As a leader you need to communicate well in both directions, to your reports and to your superiors.

In the past, I had to deal directly with a board of directors who had *not* been well informed by the previous management team. They had developed a mistrust of management, understandably, and became very high maintenance. To ultimately free up more of my time, I decided to communicate more frequently and disarm their mistrust of management. I asked my senior staff to provide a detailed weekly report of their activities, including changes to infrastructure, achievements versus goals and upcoming significant events. I then merged these reports and sent them to the board of directors every week. The daily phone calls from the directors stopped and their confidence in our management team was improved because they saw what everyone was doing and how it all came to support the company vision. The rollup was so effective I decided to send it to the entire organization. If we expect our team to understand the vision and where to add value, we need to keep them informed.

In this chapter, we've discussed three main points I believe you should revisit frequently to lead an effective organization:

- Everyone understanding the vision.
- Annual reinvention exercises.
- Effective communication.

5

Hiring, Firing and Empowerment

SAM WESTBROOK—CONSULTANT, BUS-INESSMAN, FIGHTER PILOT AND RE-TIRED BRIGADIER GENERAL: *A very senior Air Force general once told an audience that 20 percent of the people in most offices do 80 percent of the work. The reason the 20 percent don't do more is they spend the rest of their time covering for their contemporaries. More people die from boredom than from overwork. Put the challenges out there and keep book on who rises to the occasion. And debrief the ones who are not making the grade. A couple of them may wake up.*

- Hire the best.
- Eliminate the worst.
- Empower those left standing.

Hiring

Firing

Empowerment

HIRE THE BEST

JIM LATHAM—DIRECTOR, INTERNATIONAL BUSINESS DEVELOPMENT, LOCKHEED MARTIN; FIGHTER PILOT AND RETIRED BRIGADIER GENERAL: *When I was a candidate for Thunderbird Lead (the commanding position with the Air Force aerial demonstration team), there were originally nine candidates who went through interviews with the two-star general. When it was down to two of us, we took a written test of twenty questions followed by a three-and-one-half-hour interview with the four-star general. He wanted to know everything about our lives and wasn't going to risk bringing the wrong person aboard. By the end of the interview, he knew almost everything about my life. The next day he selected me for the position saying he made the final decision because I appeared to be very lucky and that he needed some luck. He was referring to the fact that when I recounted my life story I talked about several situations where I almost lost my life but was lucky and did not. He needed some luck because he had lost six jets and six pilots on the Thunderbirds in nine months.*

RANDY MEHLIN—AIRLINE PILOT, FIGHTER PILOT AND RETIRED LIEUTENANT COLONEL: *One of my commanders had a plaque in his office that exactly described the kind of people I want working for me.*

> *There go my men. I must run and catch up to them,*
> *for I am their leader.*
> **Alexandre Ledru-Rollin**

When we look at hiring the best, it is important to keep in mind it is much easier to hire than to fire. We can hire someone sight unseen or in just a matter of minutes, versus the days, weeks, or months it can take to eliminate a bad apple, plus the threat of legal action that could tie us up even longer. I'm always amazed at how little time we spend on background checks, reference checks, psychological testing and profiling, not to mention the interview process conducted with enough different people to really get to know the person. I always suggest that several individuals—the technically competent as well as those with a track record for having that gut feeling for finding the right people—be involved in the hiring process. Don't cut any corners here. Ensure you have the best possible player.

> **GENERAL (RETIRED) COLIN POWELL:** *Look for intelligence and judgment, and most critically, a capacity to anticipate, to see around corners. Also look for loyalty, integrity, a high-energy drive, a balanced ego and the drive to get things done.*

The recent economic downturn, during which most of our human resources activities centered on reducing the employee count, made us appreciate the great opportunity and optimism associated with the hiring of new team members. It also made us aware of the importance of doing our homework on those hires, in the event layoffs (and the associated legal problems) are needed again.

> **JEAN SCHLEMMER—CORPORATE EXECUTIVE:** *If you're spending all of your time managing people, you've got the wrong people. You need to hire the right people to begin with. If you inherit people, I think you have to start with figuring out what you have. What motivates them? Some people don't want to grow. They're just not interested. Well, you can't grow people who aren't interested in growing. At that point, you need to figure out, okay, are they in the right role?*

As I mentioned earlier, when I worked for John Farrish we had a policy/checkpoint that if someone had been at more than three jobs in the past five years, we'd shy away. I've seen that validated time and time again throughout my career. I'm sure you can look back at hires that floated from job to job prior to being on your team and see most of them ended up moving off your team in a similar time period.

> *"The enemies of the future are always*
> *the very nicest people."*
> **Christopher Morley, 1890–1957**

Some people just need frequent change. Others have a propensity for getting into trouble with issues ranging from the team to the customer to the law. In any case, believe me when I say you'll save yourself a lot of headaches if you always look for people who have reasonable durations in jobs across their resumes.

> *"Be not angry that you cannot make others as you wish them*
> *to be, since you cannot make yourself as you wish to be."*
> **Thomas A. Kempis, 1380–1471**

Of course, young candidates may not have had the time to establish such a record, so an alternative evaluation needs to be executed. I have a talk with them to explore long-term goals and professional expectations. Many of these younger candidates won't be sly enough to give you the pat answers. On many occasions I've had candidates share their intent to use the job opportunity as a "stepping stone" to what they really want to do long-term.

HALE BURR—CONSULTANT, FIGHTER PILOT AND RETIRED MAJOR GENERAL: *One of my commands was composed of two F-15 fighter squadrons and one T-33 squadron. The F-15 units had highly experienced pilots that I never had to worry about. In matters of discipline and mission accomplishment, these two organizations* *were extremely professional with strong squadron commanders. However, the T-33 unit was composed of forty-two of the oldest jets in the USAF. The mission of this unit was unglamorous because they flew as intercept targets for our modern fighter jets all over the continental United States. It was also a very young squadron with one lieutenant colonel as commander, a major as operations officer (# 2 ranking position in the unit), six young captains and about fifty lieutenants.*

Right after I became the wing commander, the T-33 squadron commander came up for a normal reassignment. In picking his successor, I decided I really needed strong leadership there. I selected the very best operations officer in one of the F-15 squadrons as the new T-33 commander. I called him in to tell him of my decision, realizing he really wanted to command an F-15 unit. I think his wife was more disappointed in his new position than he was. Anyway he "sucked it up," saluted and marched in the direction I had chosen for him (without any bitching or complaining that I ever heard about).

I always really admired him for being such a good soldier. He was a very charismatic forceful leader and soon had this squadron excelling in all areas—especially flying safety (that had concerned me). I always slept better knowing he was leading this young outfit. After a year or so, he was selected to command an F-15 fighter squadron and was promoted early to the rank of colonel.

You need to determine if an employee who will leave in a few years is a good fit for your team. In some situations it may be just fine; the candidate's career goals fall into your model, and in fact provide the pipeline you need in your own organization. In other circumstances, it will be paramount to find someone who isn't looking for a move but rather wants to settle into a position for the long haul, enabling you to establish the continuity needed for proper execution and relationship building.

> **JEAN SCHLEMMER—CORPORATE EXECUTIVE:** *First, you've got to have the right people. Hewlett Packard started with Hewlett and Packard sitting in a garage asking each other what they should do. And at first, they didn't know. Sony got a group of people together and actually cast about for one year trying to figure what they were going to do. Most people think you start with a vision and then you build from that. A lot of times you start with a bunch of great people and figure out what you want to do. I think if you start with great people, it's a much easier task to figure out how the company can grow.*

In the investment business I've always found it a challenge to find sales assistants who were willing to stay with the job long-term. For an investment salesperson to build a book of business that is stable and long-term, it is a challenge to have customers deal with multiple, changing sales assistants. In many cases customers deal with the sales assistants for administrative issues more than they speak to the relationship manager or salesperson.

Early on, I hired charismatic, driven, goal-oriented young people to fill these positions. The need for change and advancement typically showed itself after only a few months. This meant the hiring and interview process was taking up a significant amount of our time. We changed the job description a bit and started looking for people who had a service orientation and less desire to partake in the sales process. The sales assistant position continued to provide opportunities for those hoping for a career on the sales side, but was also stabilized with the integration of hires that had longer-term plans for the position.

DR. SANDRA DAVIS—CORPORATE EXECUTIVE, AUTHOR AND PSYCHOLOGIST: *We have not had a lot of turnover. We have often hired people near the end of their graduate school program, brought them in to learn our systems and clients. We want them to stay. But, as we've changed strategic direction, we've had some turnover because some people (who fit the earlier organization) didn't fit when we shifted direction. Those are tough conversations to have. But they are about what's best for this organization long-term. You keep respect for the individual and what they can do, but you have to be able to say:"This isn't where you can do your best work anymore." It's painful but it's best for both not to prolong a poor fit. We do what we ask our clients to do in selecting new team members. We do interviews, assessments, and reference checks to the degree we can. But finding talent is what I see as one of my top responsibilities. If we want to go from good to great, we have to surround ourselves with people who have the right talent.*

Attracting and retaining talent is one of the key responsibilities of any organizational leader. You must bring in the right talent, help people develop, retain key staff and perhaps even assure there is some turnover. Insular organizations create rather funny dynamics. Having only one group of people forever can work well, but I believe adding people with new ideas who have been in different environments is energizing.

The things we focus in hiring are: Does the candidate have the skills? Does the motivation equation look right (do the candidate's passions fit the job)? And is there a good cultural fit?

ELIMINATE THE WORST

"Some people are so fond of ill luck
that they run halfway to meet it."
Douglas William Jerrold,
1803–1857

Expect some turnover and the need to remove people. One of the most important traits found in today's leaders relates to having the courage to make the tough decisions. One area that is very difficult is the decision-making process associated with cutbacks, elimination of mediocre performers and the removal of people for cause.

From Jack Welch's book, *Jack: Straight from the Gut*: "Every year, we'd ask each of GE's businesses to rank all of their top executives. The basic concept was we forced our business leaders to differentiate their leadership. They had to identify the people in their organizations that they consider in the top 20 percent, the vital middle 70, and finally the bottom 10 percent. If there were 20 people on the management staff, we wanted to know the four in the top 20 and the two in the bottom 10—by name, position, and compensation. The underperformers generally had to go."

To have an outstanding organization, you must eliminate those who aren't a good fit. It is easy to come up with excuses to *not* deal with the situation, to keep the status quo, to accept the mediocre. This reminds me of a behavior associated with sales people where they gravitate to the easy tasks to avoid the difficult ones. Many of the day-planning systems in use today require lists of *a*, *b* and *c* tasks. People gravitate towards the easier *c* tasks because they provide a handy excuse to avoid doing the real work. In the case of sales, this often means avoiding the rejection associated with the sales process. Sales people know a certain percentage of their calls are going to be ineffective. People will say no, hang up the phone and sometimes be rude. So, instead of making those calls, less effective sales people find the time to compile prospect lists, search the Internet to find the latest industry research and deal with personal issues. In the meantime, no one is calling the prospects, making the sales, or generating the revenues. When it comes to dealing with poor performers, make it an *a* task.

DAVID FISHER—BUSINESSMAN, FINANCIAL CONSULTANT AND ENTREPRENEUR: *If "dead weight" were the ones let go, the surviving work force would be more motivated and dedicated. At one Fortune 500 Company, senior management cut about 50 percent of the work force. They should have rewarded the effective professionals while eliminating the slackers. Senior management didn't have the courage to eliminate based on specific criteria. Rather, they did across-the-board cuts and lost many really great people. The result: the surviving work force has low confidence in their senior management, no real confidence in the company's future, and no sense the company will keep them on board, based on merit. I know it's tough in a big organization to make optimal decisions when it comes to these issues. But clearly the management does not appear to be encouraging continuous improvement, or holding people accountable for specific results.*

I have a process I've used for years that combines military and corporate protocol. *First* of all, ensure your employee has had a fair shake at understanding the expectations of the job. What are the things they own and need to execute? How will you evaluate their performance? Remember any goals we set need to be specific, measurable, achievable, reasonable and timely (SMART).

When a team member is not able to accomplish the goals as communicated, I provide direct feedback about the performance, work with them to correct any deficiencies and give them some

---

time to adapt to those suggestions. I also document the meeting for future use.

> **GENERAL (RETIRED) COLIN POWELL:** *How many leaders really "walk the talk" with this stuff? Too often, people are assumed to be empty chess pieces to be moved around by grand viziers, which may explain why so many top managers immerse their calendar time in deal making, restructuring and the latest management fad. How many immerse themselves in the goal of creating an environment where the best, the brightest, the most creative are attracted, retained and, most importantly, unleashed?*

Second, assuming sufficient improvement has *not* been made, I introduce the concept that the team member may not be a good fit for the position. I make it clear that if there isn't a specific improvement in performance, in a specified time, they should look for another position—and not necessarily on this team. The prudent individual will get the message here and start the process of finding another position before being terminated.

I make it clear we should work together to find a better situation, and that I will support their efforts with a letter of recommendation so long as they pursue an alternative during the probationary period.

Third, if there has not been an improvement in performance, and they haven't found an alternative position, I eliminate them with outplacement, perhaps a severance to help them through the transition, and with a positive spin on the entire event.

Assuming we're not dealing with a "cause" situation, there isn't anything we should assume about this being a bad or incompetent individual. They just don't fit this particular position. It takes all kinds, and there is someone out there who should be a better fit. In any case, deal with it and move on. Dragging it out is a demotivator for those team members who are carrying their fair share of the productivity.

RANDY MEHLIN—AIRLINE PILOT, FIGHTER PILOT AND RETIRED LIEUTENANT COLONEL: *Folks spend a lot of time at work and with co-workers. I haven't always loved my job or the task at hand, but I have almost always enjoyed going to work. I think the boss sets the tone. Even if you are building rockets, it's not always rocket science. Don't take yourself too seriously, keep it light and find the humor in situations. Foster an attitude that humor is valued. People gravitate to leaders with that kind of attitude. There will be a time when you have to drop the hammer, but when you do be sure it's not you having a bad hair day, a pet peeve, or passing along someone else's problem.*

EMPOWER THOSE LEFT STANDING

JEAN SCHLEMMER—CORPORATE EXECUTIVE: *The thing in my career about which I'm most proud of is the night before a big announcement, I called two individuals who didn't get the "big job" at home and told them what was going to happen. I said I want you to take some time to think about what you'd like to do because you have an opportunity now to step back and say okay, "I didn't get that job. I might want to do something else. What would I like to do?"*

The next day one of them came in and said, "Okay, I think I know what I'd like to do." And I said, "You don't have to make a decision today. You just found out about it last night. You can go home if you want, but why don't you take some time to think about it?" He came back the next day and said, "This is what I want to do. I want to be your chief of staff. I know you don't really want to do the HR, administrative, etc. anyway."

I did not know this person very well, but I thought to myself, wow, he certainly knows me, because that is exactly what I need to have someone help me do. And I said I think it sounds like a wonderful idea, let's do it.

That same day the other person came in and said, "Well, I understand this other guy is going to do the chief of staff role for you." And I said yes. He said, "I guess I should have said that." I said, "Yeah, right, like that's what you really want to do, the HR, administrative stuff." I said "Come on. That isn't what your interest is. Think about what your interest is. What do you want to do?"

And he found a niche that has enabled him to become, I think, the happiest, most productive person he's ever been. He is a long-term employee at General Growth. The interesting thing about his job is that it is a job of influence, not position. By that I mean he has few people reporting to him. He has some accountability to get some things done, but it is a coordination responsibility, getting people to work together and collaborate. He said it took him a full year to figure out how to win over people through influence. And now he's one of the most powerful people in the company because he gets things done through influence, not through a position of power.

At the end of the day, it was just the right thing to do, to call somebody at home to tell them what was happening. I knew I would be talking to two very, very disappointed people. And then saying to them, figure out what you want to do. I coached one of them a little bit, but they figured what they could do, what they would be good at, and they have been two of the most successful people on my group.

To empower those individuals who are the stars of your team, you need to create an atmosphere of trust and ownership. General Westbrook tells the story after he retired of being hired to run a metals remanufacturing company in dire need of a revamp. He first had the courage to cut the employees by 50 percent, leaving a "swat" team of people who were "do it all" in attitude and experience. Once they were in place, he stood back, facilitated their buy-in to the issues at hand, and then left the solutions to them.

One particular problem involved a recycling process that left waste pooled on the plant floor. Westbrook confirmed the problem with his team on a Friday and returned the following Monday to a spotless factory floor. When empowered to find a solution, the team was motivated to do so and performed well.

RANDY MEHLIN—AIRLINE PILOT, FIGHTER PILOT AND RETIRED LIEUTENANT COLONEL: *As a general rule, I'd say there is nothing the boss should ask or assign someone to do he wouldn't do himself. Once in a while, in fact, the boss should take on a job to show we're all in the same game and all of the functions add to the success of the entire team. That will go a long way the next time there is an unpleasant task someone needs to do. On the other hand, when you give someone the responsibility for a job, give the authority and ownership to do it. You can check progress, quality, etc., without interfering or appearing to second-guess. BUT the boss is still the boss, so sometimes you need to provide additional guidance or change the course.*

It is important your team understands that not all of their innovations and proposed solutions will be effective or even adopted. There is no such thing as perfection in our teams or our businesses.

External factors will, in all likelihood, make us less effective than we anticipated in our vision and strategy sessions. Aiming at goals with a reasonable stretch will lead to some failures, but overall will drive most organizations to higher levels of long-term performance.

HALE BURR—CONSULTANT, FIGHTER PILOT AND RETIRED MAJOR GENERAL: *Give people guidance and incentive—then have a good feedback system in place. Ask lots of questions on important issues or projects to make wise decisions. It is mandatory for a smooth-running unit that you listen to your team as they carry out the leader's directions and policies.*

In the proper environment, team superstars will come up with innovative concepts. What specifically is the proper environment? Exactly how do you empower your team?

NEAL BARLOW—PROFESSOR, AIR FORCE PILOT AND COLONEL: *If a leader tells their subordinates what to do and how to do it, innovations will be hard to come by. They will be conditioned to give back exactly what they think the boss wanted. Rather, they must believe the boss has faith in them and relies on them to find solutions. An effective leader will create an atmosphere that permits team members to grow, to be innovative and to make mistakes. Rewarding the innovators will create more innovators. Subsets of your staff will see the effect and, with any luck, empower their subordinates in the same fashion. There is a productivity multiple that comes from an empowered atmosphere.*

It is important that team members be empowered to test new concepts and for the leader to understand that many of them won't pan out. The team that doesn't push the envelope will not grow to its full potential.

MARK ANDERSON—CONSULTANT, FIGHTER PILOT AND RETIRED LIEUTENANT GENERAL: *Allowing people to learn from mistakes without "crucifying" them is important. The key is distinguishing between a mistake and a crime. In this context, a crime is not just criminal activity; it's intentionally violating the rules or standards. That cannot be tolerated. But people need to feel comfortable that if they make a mistake, the boss will handle it as a learning experience and everyone benefits.*

When I take over a new organization or bring new team members aboard, I make it clear from the outset that I make plenty of mistakes and I expect everyone's help. I ask for direct feedback when someone thinks I can handle something in a better fashion. I don't want a team of people who blindly follow my thoughts without any of their own intellect applied to the problems at hand.

> *"When two men in business always agree,*
> *one of them is unnecessary."*
> **William Wrigley, Jr., 1861–1932**

GENERAL (RETIRED) COLIN POWELL: *You know the expression, "It's easier to get forgiveness than permission." Well, it's true. Good leaders don't wait for official blessing to try things out. They're prudent, not reckless. But they also realize a fact of life in most organizations: if you ask enough people for permission, you'll inevitably come up against someone who believes his job is to say "no." So the moral is, don't ask. Less effective middle managers endorse the sentiment, "If I haven't explicitly been told 'yes,' I can't do it," whereas the good ones believed, "If I haven't explicitly been told 'no,' I can." There's a world of difference between these two points of view.*

The effective leader needs to create an environment that includes respect while at the same time encourages constructive criticism and an open forum as it relates to important company decisions. The fighter pilot world is one that reflects balance in feedback and respect.

RANDY MEHLIN—AIRLINE PILOT, FIGHTER PILOT AND RETIRED LIEUTENANT COLONEL: *Even I can be successful, given the right people. Put the right people in the right job and stay out of the way. Give me a bunch of "worth-a-shit" fighter pilots, people who know right from wrong and care about doing things right, who feel bad when they screw up and are determined to be better next time. For all practical purposes they would discipline themselves and . . . man, the world is my oyster. By the way, "fighter pilot," above, is an attitude, not an Air Force specialty code.*

To give you a feel for the fighter-pilot environment, when a flight is scheduled, the scheduling division assigns a flight leader and wingmen. The day before the flight the leader will assign tasks to all flight members. Some may work on the low-level navigation portion of the mission while others prepare the practice emergency procedure of the day, and still others work up the threat assessment.

Several hours before the actual flight, a formal briefing is held. The flight leader (in charge of the mission) is in total control of format and presentation. They are responsible for the orderly flow of the flight, safety, discipline and overall effectiveness of the mission. Flight members understand there will be an opportunity for questions, and there should not be interruptions to the briefing before that time. It is a time to take notes, confirm flow and order responsibilities. The flight leader sets the tone. After all questions are addressed, last-minute items are cleaned up before stepping to the aircraft for the flight.

During the flight one is never to question the authority of the flight leader. Everyone is expected to execute their responsibilities as briefed and apply them to the effective completion of the mission. If you apply this model to the war-time missions the fighter pilots are training for, you'll be better able to understand the quest for continuous improvement and execution as close to flawless as possible.

After every mission there is a debriefing in which the flight leader goes through the entire flight step by step, maneuver by maneuver, mistake by mistake, and minute by minute. The finest flight leads recreate the entire flight from the perspective of all flight members, with a constructively critical evaluation of all aspects. This includes an honest and forthright portrayal of the flight lead's errors and areas for improvement. To maximize the learning experience, he passes the floor to the other members who, one by one, add anything the lead may not have seen.

During the debrief, rank is put away. It does not matter if the flight lead is a major and the other flight members are lieutenants or if the leader is a captain and the members are all general officers. The lead will be constructively critical of the generals, and the lieutenants should be constructively critical of the major. The situation where the flight leader is not open to feedback and does not solicit criticism is less productive.

RANDY MEHLIN—AIRLINE PILOT, FIGHTER PILOT AND RETIRED LIEUTENANT COLONEL: *One of my favorite commanders ever was Bob Watson at the 10th TFS at Hahn Air Base, Germany. Before he got the squadron, he was the operations officer, and I was a scheduler. Probably a hundred times I went to him with a problem. Once in a while he'd say, "That's not a problem, that's a challenge." But more often he'd smile and say, "Randy, there are really only two kinds of people in the world: concept people and detail people. Now I'm a con-*

---

*cept man and you're a detail man; and that is a detail."
He let me know I could do whatever I felt was best, taught
me to recognize his "pain level" and gave me a confidence
that allowed me to do a lot better job.*

*He was a boss who let you know he didn't need to make
every decision, or second guess any messes you made. Let
your people know that if it's not important, then it really
is not important. Put your priorities on a vertical scale,
not a horizontal one.*

**ROGER SCHMITT—BUSINESSMAN, FIGHTER PILOT
AND RETIRED COLONEL:** *The greatest risk is not taking
one. Nothing ventured, nothing gained. My longest lasting
learning experiences were learned from my mistakes. The
trick is to avoid making the same mistakes over and over.*

Colonel Jim Latham had flown two tours (a tour is typically
two years) with the USAF Thunderbirds when I worked with him
at Misawa Air Base, Japan. He flew as a wingman in T-38s and then
as Thunderbird Lead in the F-16. There is NO ONE more experienced in leading formations of fighters, briefing complex missions or running effective debriefs. He told me during Thunderbird debriefs that he always tried to be hardest on himself. He
created an atmosphere where all team members were expected
to point out anything and everything that would improve the
team. Despite that, when he flew with me and I was the assigned
flight lead for the mission, he was respectful of my authority,
took the feedback I shared and constructively provided me with
recommendations in return. The atmosphere was open and constructive. I was empowered to organize, lead and debrief the
flight—and, therefore, I learned more and became a more valuable
resource to his organization.

NEAL BARLOW—PROFESSOR, AIR FORCE PILOT AND COLONEL: *I've always felt one of my responsibilities as a commander is to recognize the strengths of everybody who works for me. How do I do that? By setting challenging expectations and then empowering them to make their own decisions and to implement their plans. I find out not only the potential of each person, but also the cumulative capabilities of the organization. Empowerment is absolutely critical. If you fail to empower your people, you will not see innovative solutions.*

A one-liner you may want to take away from this is that "in order to be a flight lead you must first prove yourself as an effective wingman." In the fighter pilot world, one starts at the bottom of the totem pole and works up. Some will never be more than wingmen, some will advance to be air-to-ground flight leads, others will be air-to-air flight leads, and still others will be mission commanders responsible for flights of dozens of aircraft. Not everyone advances to the top of the totem pole.

JEAN SCHLEMMER—CORPORATE EXECUTIVE: *I'm very much a hands-off manager, which is why it is so important to have the right people in the right seats on the bus. I like to set an end goal and then let people figure out how to get there. General George Patton said, "Never tell people how to do things. Tell them what to do, and they will surprise you with their ingenuity." To say nothing about their creativity. So instead of me telling my staff where and how we're going somewhere, I'm much more likely to say, "Here's where we're going; figure out the best way to get there. Call me if you need help. Especially call me before you slide into the ditch, and it takes two tow trucks to pull you out."*

The most effective units I've been involved with have a team where everyone focuses on their assigned tasks, no matter what they might entail, and does their utmost to perform those tasks flawlessly. The brand-spanking-new lieutenants ended up with the less glamorous jobs in the fighter squadron. The "snacko," for example, had to ensure the snack bar and coolers were properly stocked with the appropriate snacks and beverages. This may not be the most enticing assignment for a recent hotshot graduate. However, if the lieutenant did a less than outstanding job as snacko, it was an indication of his commitment to mission. The team member who goes the extra mile is the team member who will advance in responsibility. Can-do attitudes and relentless pursuit of improvement are what you need on your team. Find those people, train them, reinforce them and move them into positions of responsibility with a license to get the job done.

HALE BURR—CONSULTANT, FIGHTER PILOT AND RETIRED MAJOR GENERAL: *When two of my fighter wings were selected to compete in an Air Force worldwide aerial gunnery competition, I had the responsibility to select the team members. For a variety of complicated operational reasons, I picked very junior fighter squadron flight commanders as the team leaders instead of more senior officers. At that time, each of them happened to be the best and most outstanding flight commanders in the Wing. Both times, I called these young officers in and empowered them to make all the arrangements for the team. They had both the responsibility and authority to pull together a team, set up the training schedule and ensure the operational success and safety in going to these prestigious contests.*

Of course I asked all the right questions to make sure it went the right way, but I certainly did not meddle with what they chose to do in meeting the mission I assigned to them. Those key questions tweaked the operation to make it just what we needed to get the job done in a professionally outstanding manner. No micromanaging but some gentle steering. My wing did not win either gunnery meet (we came in second and fourth) but those young flight commanders and their teams gave it their best shot. Much later, both of these young officers were promoted to be general officers. Hopefully this experience helped them in service to the Air Force and this great county of ours.

I admit it is uncommon, particularly in the corporate world, to work with leaders who encourage feedback and criticism of their performance. Many senior executives are defensive about their authority and reluctant to take feedback that might reflect negatively upon their position and ability. I believe this to be an enormous mistake that cripples the organization. It is up to the leader to open the doors for improvement and constructive feedback. Most subordinates will not (and probably should not) provide recommendations for improvement to a manager who does not encourage it. It takes a very confident and high-performance team to openly provide constructive feedback across the boundaries created by the superior-subordinate paradigm we live with. However, if you have a group that provides respectful and constructive feedback and doesn't feel intimidated to do so, then I think you are doing a pretty good job at empowering your team!

SAM WESTBROOK—CONSULTANT, BUSINESSMAN, FIGHTER PILOT AND RETIRED BRIGADIER GENERAL:
I once stood in front of my command and told them I'd heard a rumor going around suggesting I could do the job of ten people. I told them, "Although I'm flattered you think so, I'd like to point out there are over 5,000 jobs in this organization, and, even if you are right about the ten, I'll be unable to cover the remaining 4,990 positions."

If we want the most out of a team, we must empower them to take some chances and expect them to take feedback from their team members, with an appetite for continuous improvement in their responsibilities. At the same time, it is a rare situation where the solutions of one are better than the collective problem-solving power of many.

JEAN SCHLEMMER—CORPORATE EXECUTIVE: *I care less about what we do right now. I care about how we're doing it and who is doing it. The genetic code for our company has little to do with the functional skills. When we talk about putting our CFO on the company spaceship, it's not because he's got financial skills, it's because he's got leadership qualities and talent and management skills and characteristics and attributes beyond the functional skills.*

One of the great benefits of the annual reinvention exercise is the chance to take team members from the lowest levels, give them as much input as anyone else, and then hear their perspective on where and how the company should proceed. I'm always pleased with the many great ideas and improvements to the company business plan that come from team members otherwise kept silent by the organizational chart. Create an atmosphere where all the team members know they are expected to challenge you if they see something going the wrong direction and offer up ideas, no matter how out of the box they may appear.

Don't shortchange the time and effort you need to find the right people. If you do, you'll waste a great deal more time dealing with employee issues. When you find employees who aren't the right fit, deal with them quickly and fairly. Once you've got the team put together—and this is an endless exercise—be sure to allow mistakes and encourage risk taking for the sake of the organization.

Lessons to take away from this chapter include:
- Hire the best.
- Eliminate the worst.
- Empower those left standing.

ENSURING ACCOUNTABILITY

"I simply do not have the time, nor inclination, to distinguish between the incompetent and the unlucky."
General Curtis Lemay

In this chapter, let us

- Set expectations.
- Get into the details.
- Have the courage to apply the consequences.

SET EXPECTATIONS

When I was in the Investment Division of Norwest Corporation, I worked with some outstanding individuals. There were many different leadership styles in the group. One regional sales manager was talented at setting expectations. Reporting to her was an institutional sales person who was about as

Expectations

Details

Courage

pleasant as you can imagine. Always friendly, never too outgoing or obnoxious, and always made his goals—just! This regional sales manager recognized that whatever the total revenue goal had been, the sales person barely made it, but he did always make it! Previous managers had allowed him to barter for a "mediocre" revenue target.

Some of us are naturally motivated to always try to grow our productivity, whether raising turnips or generating sales commissions. This particular employee did not have internal drive. So, his manager increased his revenue target, year after year, and no longer accepted the level production goals acceptable in years past. Although he never exceeded his goal by more than a few percent, his production more than doubled in a matter of a few years.

BUZ BAXTER—BUSINESSMAN, FIGHTER PILOT AND RETIRED MAJOR GENERAL: *Most workers can improve the quality and quantity of their production if they are encouraged and expected to do so. Leaders need to learn that most subordinates will not do more than is demanded of them, although they usually have the capacity to do more or better than is expected of them.*

I think of employee goal-setting sessions as negotiations. Let's sit down and look at your history, do a revenue growth fit to the history, and then see if we can stretch it a bit. This will be good for the company and good for your income. In fact, I often put an additional bonus incentive on top of the regular commission schedule to motivate a "stretch."

You are probably familiar with what is called the "Pygmalion" effect. For a leader it is the ability to take someone to a higher level and make them believe in themselves, to take a team member and get above-average results. How do you motivate someone to perform beyond their expectations and history? I think it starts in the setting of goals and expectations.

JOHN FARRISH—CORPORATE EXECUTIVE: *If I have the expectation and the person doesn't buy into it, it doesn't mean anything to them. So I have to make sure we have the same understanding of what the expectations are. And then it's ongoing feedback and, as somebody once said, inspecting what you expect. It's not only staying on top of what's happening, not from the point of view of my making a decision, but understanding the results are coming from the manager's time and energy. But it's also continuing to communicate during that period of time about my perceptions and their perceptions. And I find the biggest compliment I can get about expectations and accountability is when I sit down with somebody and they know exactly how they're doing—and my point of view and theirs is the same because we've been clear in our communications.*

I went through a period, early in my flying career, where expectations had *not* been clearly laid out for me. In an interview, General John Lorber shared the following:

JOHN LORBER—VICE PRESIDENT, BOEING SPACE AND COMMUNICATIONS OPERATIONS AND RETIRED GENERAL: *One of the most interesting stories I've heard was from a friend who was telling me about a time when they had a group of pilots who found it fun to fly underneath bridges. My friend was brought in front of the squadron commander one day who said, "There's a rumor some of you pilots are flying underneath bridges. I'm not going to ask you if you have flown underneath a bridge, I just want to tell you—I want my fighter pilots to want to fly underneath the bridge but have the self-discipline not to."*

It is an interesting way to look at the need to both instill fighter pilot spirit, as well as the discipline. It lets your people know exactly what is expected of them.

I asked General Lorber why he had waited twenty years to share the story with me. It might have proven useful to me as I was considering doing a 700 mile-per-hour fly-by of my aunt's house!

ROGER SCHMITT—BUSINESSMAN, FIGHTER PILOT AND RETIRED COLONEL: *To be fair and objective, goal setting should be a contract between two parties in agreement of what is expected. I have most enjoyed working for people who set tough standards and enforce them fairly.*

I used to talk with my sales people about what it might be like to produce a million dollars of revenue for the company. I enjoyed planting the seed and getting them to imagine how their lifestyle would change and how their assessment of self worth would differ. "So, Chris, imagine if you'd done the same production as Matt. He took home $550,000 in commissions this year. How would your life change with a ten-fold increase in income?" I liked to wait for the sales person to ask for suggestions on how we might get their productivity up to the same levels as our top producers. At that point it is back to Chapter 4 and our discussion on backing down into the details from the overall goal: Vision, Strategy, Tactics and Commitment.

SAM WESTBROOK—CONSULTANT, BUSINESSMAN, FIGHTER PILOT AND RETIRED BRIGADIER GENERAL: *Communicate expectations, set parameters and metrics, give regular feedback (which almost nobody does regularly or well—it is an art) and be consistent.*

Most successful sales people have figured out it is simply a matter of keeping the right activity at a high enough level. A little luck can accelerate the process but only if you are prepared for the opportunities.

GET THE DETAILS

From Jack Welch's book, *Jack: Straight from the Gut*: "There are advantages to being the chairman.

"One of my favorite perks was picking out an issue and doing what I called a 'deep dive.' It's spotting a challenge where you think you can make a difference—one that looks like it would be fun—and then throwing the weight of your position behind it. Some might justifiably call it 'meddling.'

"I've done this—just about everywhere in the company.

"I got involved in everything my nose told me to get involved in, from the quality of our X-ray tubes to the introduction of gem-quality diamonds. I picked my shots and took the dive. I was doing this up until my last days in the job."

To have credibility with your team you need to understand the details, be conversant in process and product and preferably have some personal experience in the trenches.

JEAN SCHLEMMER—CORPORATE EXECUTIVE: *You're not empowering anybody if you're looking over their shoulder all the time.*

One of my favorite phrases is "empowerment without support is abandonment." You have to support them, but that doesn't mean you have to micro-manage them. It gets back to if you know them, if you know how they're wired, if you know how they think, ultimately it gets to trust. If you don't trust the people you've got doing the work, my first question is, whose fault is that? You hired them, and if you don't trust them, what does that say about you?

Andrew Carnegie's epitaph is "Here lies the body of a man

whose one talent is that he hired people better than he is."
That's what I want my epitaph to be. I hope my talent is
that I can pick a group of really, really talented people to
actually do the business of running our business.

Back to the details. At the end of the day, the operating
results of the company are my responsibility. So do I get
into the details of that? You bet. Does that mean I get
down to the nitty-gritty of a line item in a property?
Probably not. But I sure understand every line item on
my financial statement and what it means.

Some of the finest squadron commanders I ever worked for would routinely fly training missions with the squadron pilots. They knew how their pilots flew, understood the challenges of the mission and carried a higher credibility with the team.

"As a senior leader, you need to have the discipline to get
micro-knowledge and the courage not to micro-manage."
Author Unknown

A technique I still use today is to have a weekly written summary from all of the company divisions. This is, in effect, an accountability system that also keeps me up to date on what everyone in the company is doing. On the one hand, I can compare the senior level summaries to our company strategy and catch nonperformance while there is time to correct or accelerate. On the other hand, I know enough details to be conversant with everyone in the organization. I make an effort to walk around and touch base with people as often as I can. I ask them about their specific goals and accomplishments and try to comment on any details I might have picked up in the weekly summary. I think this keeps everyone on their toes but more important, shows I know and care about the details of their job.

DR. SANDRA DAVIS—CORPORATE EXECUTIVE, AUTHOR AND PSYCHOLOGIST: *We all want and need course correction: positive and negative feedback. Most senior leaders don't understand the degree of detail people need to know how well they're performing. A person needs to hear specifics. Otherwise, how do they know what to repeat? Since most executives will focus on strategy and vision, and they're thinking at 50,000 feet, they assume that other people can translate the vision into the specifics. That assumption is dangerous.*

So the person at the top needs to be into the details of behavioral feedback in a way that they may acknowledge at some level, but not fully understand. It may mean saying to someone, "You know the presentation you did yesterday for this particular customer worked well. What I really liked is you came in with materials that fit them. You listened to what their needs were and crafted something on the spot. That was fabulous. Do it the next time you go out and meet with someone." That's the level of detailed feedback people need to hear.

HAVE THE COURAGE TO APPLY THE CONSEQUENCES

Here's where the rubber hits the road. In my estimation, many leaders and managers in corporate America and the military don't have the courage to make tough decisions. When it comes to making decisions for the good of the organization and the personal lives of employees, we tend to wimp out.

Don't get me wrong. I think most Fortune 500 companies have someone at the helm who is willing to make these decisions. But the great majority of leadership and senior staff count on the top leader to make those decisions, especially regarding personnel. It is much easier, albeit still painful, to go to your team and say, "Our

CEO has decided . . . and therefore we'll be seeing a reduction in staff. I fought it as hard as I could but they made up their mind."

It's possible that organizations with a strong leader will survive, despite the senior staff not wanting to make the tough decisions, as long as the top dog drives it down. However, anyone not willing to make the tough decisions, painful as they may be, is not focused on the right things.

What this often leads to is a great decision for the balance sheet but weak implementation by those closest to the employees. Large corporations have made the proper decision to reduce their employee force, but ended up losing their strongest players and keeping the weakest. Their management staff lacked the courage to eliminate the weakest links. Seeing no accountability or leadership, the stronger players got frustrated and left. Leadership should permeate the organization and the decision to retain or release should be made at the lowest possible level, with the decision being a business decision versus a personal cop out.

I admit to feeling pain every time I have to let someone go, no matter what the reason. Every employee is a human being trying to make a go at a decent lifestyle, and many have families they are caring for. If a leader doesn't feel any pain, then I question their ability to truly care about and effectively lead their team.

In my military days, there was often a significant consequence to not making the tough decisions—in particular, not eliminating weak pilots. In a combat situation, there needs to be a minimum competence in order to survive. If the low-performance pilots were not eliminated from the fighter world, they would sometimes end up killing themselves and taking someone else with them.

JIM LATHAM—DIRECTOR, INTERNATIONAL BUSINESS DEVELOPMENT, LOCKHEED MARTIN; FIGHTER PILOT AND RETIRED BRIGADIER GENERAL: *Probably one of the biggest mistakes I ever made related to an* individual in one of my squadrons. He ran low on gas, and when he came back, he did not declare to the tower he had emergency fuel—which would have given him priority landing. He didn't say anything and landed with just enough gas to taxi to the ramp. It was only after the crew chief filled the almost-dry airplane tank with gas that I confronted him with it, and he admitted to it. But he was a good pilot. I had kind of a philosophy that I had learned from someone else in the aviation business that 15 percent of your pilots are going to do 90 percent of the battle damage. They're going to do 90 percent of the effort. There are always just a few really outstanding people who you are going to need in battle. And so, I felt this kid was worth nursing along.

This young pilot had another incident where he was using the afterburner in the traffic pattern when we were at deployed location. Not violating anything, but using bad judgment, I called him on the carpet. And then he had another incident I witnessed where he violated the rules of engagement during air-to-air combat in the training environment. This was the third one!

I almost took the step of convening a flying evaluation board, which would have made a decision whether this individual would keep his wings and continue flying in the Air Force. My gut feeling was we probably ought to get rid of this guy, but I still hung onto this other side of me that said he would come around if we keep with him. So when we closed this particular squadron down, I had to assign these guys to their next aircraft. I assigned him to be an instructor because I felt if he could ride in the backseat of others less talented than he, he would learn that not everybody flies as well as he does. Therefore, as *a leader, in the future he would have to take into account the weakest link in his flight when we decide what they're going to go do. And not everybody can do things as aggressively as he can and get away with it.*

Boy, was this pilot upset. He became an instructor, but then got out of the Air Force and joined an Air Force Reserve unit. Within a year he was out flying a low-level mission with another aviator in the backseat of a two-seat F16—and flew it into the ground. He was doing some aggressive flying and killed them both.

I've always looked back and thought, here is a guy that had a character problem. I saw it and should have taken the action at the right time to have him go do something else than fly Air Force airplanes. There is a little integrity in there, but it's more of a character issue. I think we as senior leaders have a responsibility to look for these kinds of characteristics and make the tough decision when the decision has to be made.

In one of my corporate management roles, I was confronted with a challenging personnel issue. The top producer in the office, responsible for much of the total revenue production in an office of ten sales people, was absolutely out of control. His personal life was a mess, he was right on the limit when it came to compliance with regulations, and he held the office hostage with his self-centered behavior. His integrity was an issue with both customers and fellow employees.

This employee had been with the company for more than a decade and had relationships with the most lucrative of our customer base. Nonetheless, I had to talk frankly with him about his behavior and my concerns. I tried to use the sandwich approach, sharing my admiration for his production, followed by my concerns from a compliance and personnel standpoint, and finally my desire to work with him in overcoming these concerns. He blew a cork!—screaming and falling onto the floor in the fetal position, where he wept. I knew I had a big problem. (The previous sentence defines "understatement"!)

Senior corporate management had in the past ignored this employee's behavior. His evaluations had all included top rankings because of his financial contribution to the company. He was clearly in need of help. Because this was one of our first meetings and I had no paper trail, I needed some time to assess and document the situation. He went to a medical facility for some help, brought me the doctor's comments and calmed down for a while.

A month later I followed up with the doctor and found the individual had falsified the comments. He hadn't made any of the doctor visits he'd claimed and had written the "doctor's comments" himself. When I confronted him with the facts, he came across my desk and physically threatened me, saying I'd be removed for taking on such a senior person. At that point, there was no doubt I needed to remove him, and I did.

The office personnel were frightened enough by the man's behavior that we hired an armed guard to sit in our lobby for a couple of weeks until we heard the terminated employee had moved to another state. I learned that his pattern continued with subsequent employers. Clearly, I had done the right thing. My action was reinforced not only by his continuing behavior but also by information that came to us after the fact. He was involved in serious chemical abuse problems as well as other illegal activities.

The hostile work environment that had existed was corrected, and we made up the lost revenue in short order. I became known throughout the company because I had terminated a top producer. I wasn't happy to do it, but was pleased to have found the courage to take the proper action.

HALE BURR—CONSULTANT, FIGHTER PILOT AND RETIRED MAJOR GENERAL: *Have courage—Everyone possesses varying amounts of physical courage. However, what is most important for leaders is MORAL courage.You have to be able to look people straight in the eye and tell them the hard truth. This is hard because it affects their careers, families and lives. Accept responsibility for making the right decision, not the easy, politically correct one.*

At the risk of being redundant, I want to reinforce my belief that you aren't going to change people. If you have a bad apple, don't spend too much time trying to correct their behavior, particularly with seasoned people. If you don't believe me, take a look at some of the people you've eliminated and see what they did with the rest of their lives. If someone has a poor work ethic, it will likely continue. Exceptions are for a young team member who had the wrong boss and wasn't exposed to the tutelage and example needed for proper development. There are exceptions, but for the most part these employees are going to hang on to the traits they've picked up throughout their careers. Clean up the team and move on.

NEAL BARLOW—PROFESSOR, AIR FORCE PILOT AND COLONEL: *If you have someone not living up to your expectations, you have to address that immediately. It doesn't necessarily have to be a put-down or to be negative. Sometimes you can take a person who is not performing up to your standards, or who is not on board, and turn them around with daily accountability.*

There are also times where you need to countermand decisions made by your senior staff, if they aren't in the best interest of the team. This is difficult because we're talking about the staff you need to trust and empower. Nonetheless, there are times when you need to look them in the eye and say, "Poor decision, I'm overriding it!"

JIM LATHAM—DIRECTOR, INTERNATIONAL BUSINESS DEVELOPMENT, LOCKHEED MARTIN; FIGHTER PILOT AND RETIRED BRIGADIER GENERAL: *I can cite one more example of having to make those tough decisions. This was at Misawa, Japan. We had taken a deployment to Alaska to participate in an exercise there. And I was going to be the senior guy, but there was this squadron commander who was actually in charge of the operations. I attended his predeployment briefings where he talked to all the maintenance folks, all the people who are going on the deployment. He kind of laid the ground rules; part of it was about behavior. He said, "If you're going to get in trouble, you can plan on being sent home." Well, we made the deployment up there and got in about 11 P.M., in the summer. It's still daylight so the guys go off and have some fun. And apparently some of the officers got a little rambunctious, the cops were called and several of them were hauled in.*

I attended the first meeting the next morning for our in-briefing for the exercise. The host commander stood up and said, "Well, I guess you guys got into a little trouble last night." This was the first I knew of it, and I'm sitting right beside the squadron commander "What's the deal?" I ask. He said, "Oh, it's not a big deal." Later, I sat down with him and asked what had happened, and what he planned to do about it? And he said, "Well, I think I'll ground them for a couple days, make my point and then they'll continue to participate in the exercise."

And I said, "I sat in your briefing for all your maintenance guys when you said if you get in trouble while you're on this deployment, you're going home." And he said, "Yeah I said that, but these guys are pilots, this

*whole deployment is for their training, and if we send
them home, then they're not going to get the value of the
training." I asked him to think about that again and
reconsider it. He didn't change his mind. In this situation
I overrode him, stepped in what I thought was a bad decision and sent five of the pilots home. Very significant
impact to them as they really wanted to be in the exercise.*

*I was treated with some disrespect (despite the fact I was
the wing commander) by the squadron commander and
by four of those five guys for the rest of the time that we
were there. But, when we got back home, one individual
made an appointment and sat down and said, "Colonel
Latham, I screwed up. I was wrong and you did the right
thing, and I just don't want you to hold it against me. I
made a mistake and I want to better myself with you in
the time we have remaining here at Misawa." And he did!
That young man was one of the guys I ended up mentoring and looking after. He continues his career to this
day in more responsible positions in the Air Force.*

I think it is common for all of us to want our team to like us. It
is not comfortable to lead a team where some of the members
show disrespect or a lack of support when you are trying to take
the company, squadron or team to a higher plateau. That's just part
of the job.

**BUZ BAXTER—BUSINESSMAN, FIGHTER PILOT AND
RETIRED MAJOR GENERAL:** *Differential awards based
on differential performance. Not everyone gets the same
reward—pay for performance. Trying to get everyone to
like you—NOT possible or necessary. Follow through and
have the courage. SET THE EXAMPLE. Hold everyone
accountable for meeting expectations. Never be unreasonable, but puny excuses are worse than no excuse. That said,*

good reasons for failure do occur, and the good leader must recognize not every bad situation is controllable ... acts of God do occur. It's much better to produce results than to depend on your good luck.

It was my job to take the personnel counts down some 25 percent for the survival of a company. The 75 percent that remained would also have lost their jobs had I not made the decision to cut the 25 percent. As Mr. Spock of Star Trek would say, "The needs of the many outweigh the needs of the few." Don't worry, I'm not going socialist on you, but clearly it doesn't make sense to avoid the tough decisions at the expense of the entire organization. At the same time I had to remove some of the personnel, I promoted others and increased their compensation. I choose not to live in a world of grays; I choose to live in a world of differentiation. Pay for performance but eliminate the nonproductive, uncorrectable "paper weights" that can be found in any company and on most teams.

GENERAL (RETIRED) COLIN POWELL: *Good leadership involves responsibility to the welfare of the group, which means that some people will get angry at your actions and decisions. It's inevitable, if you're honorable. Trying to get everyone to like you is a sign of mediocrity. You'll avoid the tough decisions. You'll avoid confronting the people who need to be confronted, and you'll avoid offering differential rewards based on differential performance because some people might get upset. Ironically, by procrastinating on the difficult choices, by trying not to get anyone mad, and by treating everyone equally "nicely," regardless of their contributions, you'll simply ensure that the only people you'll wind up angering are the most creative and productive people in the organization.*

So, as it relates to Accountability:

- Set expectations.
- Get into the details.
- Have the courage to apply the consequences.

ATMOSPHERE

In this section, focused on Atmosphere, we'll look at:

- Positive Thinking,
- Giving Credit, and
- Generating Enthusiasm.

7

POSITIVE THINKING

In this chapter, we'll look at the benefits of a positive work environment:
- Momentum and the Positive Motivation Model.
- Why die all tensed up?
- Deal with naysayers.

"A positive attitude may not solve all your problems, but it will annoy enough people to make it worth the effort."
Herm Albright, 1876–1944

MOMENTUM AND THE POSITIVE MOTIVATION MODEL

MARK ANDERSON—CONSULTANT, FIGHTER PILOT AND RETIRED LIEUTENANT GENERAL: *The Positive Motivation Model suggests that training will be more effective if leaders find*

Positive Motivational Model

Tensed Up?

Naysayers

strengths, provide constructive criticism and use positive rein-
forcement with their trainees, rather than relying on fear,
sarcasm and ridicule, as was commonplace in past military
training.

I had first-hand experience using the Positive Motivation
Model at the Air Force Academy in the mid '80s when I was
commandant of cadets. We wanted to get away from the tra-
ditional "yelling in the face" of new cadets by upper classmen
and making them do push-ups at the drop of a hat. It worked,
albeit with a fair amount of resistance. And with some mod-
ifications, it's still in use today.

The momentum created by a positive work environment is
crucial to both the short-term and long-term success of an organization. Recently, a prospective hire asked one of my direct reports
what it was like to work in "Bob's World." Their response was overall complimentary, with one criticism that I was overly positive. I
won't fault him for this comment; in fact, I'm pleased he noticed. I
have chosen to travel the path of optimism and to do my best to
keep a positive attitude—no matter what. I don't always achieve
this. We're all human and at times the hill does appear to be very
steep. When it does, and when I fade towards any pessimism, I min-
imize my exposure to the team.

**SAM WESTBROOK—CONSULTANT, BUSINESSMAN,
FIGHTER PILOT AND RETIRED BRIGADIER GENERAL:**
Be consistent so people know when you are being posi-
tive. It is possible to be stern and be positive at the same
time, but bouncing off the stops makes it difficult to
know where the norm is. Having balance and stamina
almost always translates into being positive. Work on the
balance and get out of the inner office where your atti-
tude can be seen and let it rub off on others.

To me, the psychology associated with the positive or negative environment is compelling. I once watched an instructor pull a student to the front of a seminar. She asked him to hold a heavy weight at arm's length for as long as he could. He held it up for just a few seconds. She then asked him to imagine the object was only half its original weight and to picture others helping him hold up the object. He proceeded to hold the weight, once again at arm's length, for more than double the original time. A positive, can-do attitude does make a difference.

DR. SANDRA DAVIS—CORPORATE EXECUTIVE, AUTHOR AND PSYCHOLOGIST: *My business was twenty years old in November 2002. We now have twenty-three staff members. Someone said to me you have really built something successful. You must be really proud. People tell us we have a great reputation, which I feel incredibly good about. But you know what I really feel good about? I feel good about the soon-to-be-retiring staff member who walked in the other day and said, "In all my career, I have never worked in a place I felt so respected. And I can't thank you enough for that experience at the end of my career."*

That is success. Yes, I want the other wins too. I want the revenue gains, the profitability, and the big contracts. I want to be able to say, " Look at the kind of impact we've had as an organization." Yes, I want that. But I also love it when someone asks, "Do you know what this organization is like for me? I've never worked anywhere like this. What a great place for me to end my career." Or when someone says, "I love to come to work in the morning." Isn't that cool? Wouldn't you love to have an organization full of people who love to come to work in the morning?

People in my business, the consulting world, psychologists or others, frequently do a lot of work in organizations to help improve the atmosphere, climate and culture. But they rarely look in their own backyard. When we founded this business, my partner and I decided we wanted to build an internal environment that is as good as what we're trying to create for our clients. That's the legacy. At some point, most leaders think about the legacy they want to leave. I hope to leave this organization with strong, talented people who are good at what they do and who work together with a sense of team and respect for each other. The legacy will be that they feel this is a great place to work.

Some leaders go overboard on setting out challenges. One leader I recall assumed he needed to be tough as a leader. He defined his job as accountability, tough-minded goals, pushing people and making them work hard. Every time people didn't reach their goals, he highlighted their mistakes. Rather than getting the high performance he sought, people became incredibly de-motivated.

So where am I on the optimism scale? Sort of relentlessly optimistic! I truly believe we will achieve certain things. We will make certain things happen. And people need to hear that. They need to hear that the leader believes in the future. Can you ever say, "This is a struggle, this isn't the easiest time?" Sure, there are times when I wake up at night and think, "Can we really do this?" But, I end up absolutely believing in what it is we are doing. We can do this. We can make this happen. And we've hired some people who multiply that enthusiasm. We deliberately brought in someone this year who matches my level of optimism and enthusiasm. We needed more of that this year because of the difficult economic climate.

There is a psychological principle. Have you ever heard of something called "learned optimism" or "learned helplessness?" Do you believe you're the master of your fate or do you believe the world around you controls you? In this small business one of the things I look for in adding leaders to our group is people who believe they're the masters of their own fate. That level of belief and momentum will help the business move forward. Do you believe you can affect your own destiny or are you carried by the whims of whatever is out there?

You need a certain critical mass of people who believe they're the masters of their own fate to carry the business forward. And if it's only in you as the leader, well that's tough. Without that you can feel like you're pushing a rope because it's not moving along on its own.

When I taught at Holloman Air Force Base, we employed a now-archaic system where we'd use 16mm film cartridges for filming through the heads-up display. Whenever we pushed the bomb drop button or squeezed the gun trigger, the film would turn on and run for a few seconds. After the flight, we would analyze the film for the sake of training and continuous improvement.

The AT-38 we used for air combat training was a lot of fun. However, it didn't carry much fuel. Since most air-to-air flights were flown at maximum power, utilizing the afterburner, it was typical to spend only minutes in the practice area. On a typical mission flown to practice offensive maneuvers, one might use up half of the 16mm film. It was virtually impossible to use all of the film available in a cartridge.

Every now and then we'd get the opportunity to fly without students to practice basic fighter maneuvering skills against other instructors. Psychology was a major factor on these sorties. A confident briefing followed by properly placed confirmations of one's ability could "win the fight before we took off." When I first heard this concept I found it suspect. However, it was confirmed to me, time and time again.

Of the 200 instructor pilots at the fighter lead-in course, six were chosen to be flight examiners. If ever there was a flight to be dreaded, it was a check ride with a flight examiner.

By the time I took on the flight examiner role, I'd taken the "psychology of the fight" to a higher plateau. Wearing the black scarf of a flight examiner was a good start since most instructors wanted to ensure a positive relationship and were intimidated by the situation, whether it was a check ride or a continuation and training flight.

As I pointed out, it was virtually impossible to use all of a film pack on a single flight. If you were always on the offense, always taking the simulated gun and missile shots, you still couldn't use more than one cartridge.

The ride to the airplane in a crew van was the last direct opportunity to affect the psychology of the mission. I found it useful to carry two film cartridges in clear view of my opponent. It was humorous to see the other instructor digest the suggestion I'd be shooting him so often I would have to switch to a second cartridge. He'd then look me in the eye to see if I was serious. I refused to even blink; this was war! It was very effective. I was clearly confident about what I was going to do during the competition. Opponents couldn't shake the thought, which detracted from their overall situational awareness and gave me an advantage. As most fighter pilots will tell you, "I can't ever remember losing a fight."

> *"Why not? is a slogan for an interesting life."*
> **Mason Cooley**

The same strategy can be applied in business. If you are in a competitive situation for a business opportunity, going in with a positive attitude makes it more likely you'll get the business. If you were the decision maker, whom would you select? The company carrying the extra film cartridge or the competition that just got a migraine at the thought of having to compete against such a confident adversary?

RANDY MEHLIN—AIRLINE PILOT, FIGHTER PILOT AND RETIRED LIEUTENANT COLONEL: *One of the best speakers I've ever heard gave a great lecture about fairness. He said he'd been out to dinner the night before with a doctor and his wife when the guy at the next table began to choke on a piece of steak. He asked the doctor if he was going to help do the Heimlich maneuver or something! He said he would but it wouldn't be fair to the rest of the people in the restaurant because he didn't have time to do the Heimlich to the rest of them.*

The speaker pointed out that a large part of fairness is not to give everyone the same thing, but to try to give each what they need. I disliked working for or with people whose going-in position was, " You can't please everyone." I always thought the unspoken part was, "So I'm not going to try."

I once worked for a colonel who said he hired me because of my presence and positive effect. When I walked into a room, my demeanor suggested that whatever the task, I'd get it done and whatever the problems, I'd overcome. If you don't feel you portray this confidence, then I suggest you change your behavior and make your best effort towards turning any situation into a positive with a "can-do" attitude.

> *"The man who can't dance thinks the band is no good."*
> ***Polish Proverb***

There is a difference between arrogance and confidence. The proper display of confidence is one that includes some humility.

When asked whether you can do something, do you reply, "Of course, perhaps you've heard of me?" or, "I don't know, but I'll be giving it my best!" Internally, you need to be certain about yourself, but the words need to reflect humility, drive and your dedication to completing the task at hand. Let your results confirm your ability to get things done.

NEAL BARLOW—PROFESSOR, AIR FORCE PILOT AND COLONEL: *I do enjoy working with the aeronautical engineering program, and I enjoy working with the flying program here. We are trying to bring the introductory flying program back here to the Academy. And in all those things, I get to be positive about what we are trying to do. I'm also the high school's women's assistant basketball coach. I get to be positive in that environment as well. A study at UCLA looked at coaches who tended to be positive with their players. It also looked at coaches who were always telling you what you did wrong, and why you weren't meeting the expectation they had. Finally, it looked at the coaches that had a blending of the two.*

From my experiences, I think it is important to be positive, but also at times, there must be consequences when your team members chose to not do the right things. This study shows that at all times it was the positive coach who was the most successful. That doesn't mean you sugarcoat it and tell a person they are wonderful, even when they do a bad job. But you should always find something positive about them or about something they are trying to do. Then reinforce that positive thing to try and correct the negative thing they are doing. A leader who is able to put things positively is

*able to move forward in a way that is going to be far
more successful.*

Don't you agree that while we all believe in our profession, we work hard to be successful, and we want our organization to do great things, nonetheless, the bottom line continues to be our enjoying life? And, if we don't enjoy living, and we don't give our subordinates a good opportunity to enjoy what they do, why is it we want to live on this earth?

> *"There is no cure for birth and death,
> save to enjoy the interval."*
> **George Santayana, 1863–1952**

JEAN SCHLEMMER—CORPORATE EXECUTIVE: *There is no future in negativism. I think the theory is that people who respond to fear and negativism are people who will do one thing well, over and over and over. But people who are positive and people who are in a positive environment will do a lot of things better. I'm known as one of the most positive persons in my company—the company cheerleader. It's just the way I'm wired. I think positive atmospheres come from positive people. And I don't know how else you create a positive environment unless you have positive people. Positive actions and behavior come naturally from positive people. I think it is just how people are wired, how they get up in the morning, whether they're happy to be alive. Happiness is an inside job. You are the only person who can put it there and keep it there. It's nobody else's job, just as it's not your job to make anybody else happy. And that's how you should live.*

Leo Broline went to college in Colorado and graduated with a degree in aeronautical engineering. He joined the Air Force, flew F-4 Phantoms in North Carolina and Iceland, and then proceeded to instruct at the Air Force fighter lead-in course at Holloman Air Force Base, New Mexico. Leo got out of the Air Force for a couple of years and flew as a test pilot for Mitsubishi. In 1981 he became an instructor at Holloman, where we first met.

Leo was a brilliant individual, driven to achieve while, at the same time, determined to make a positive situation out of anything that could be perceived as negative. Leo had an incredible ability to put mind over matter. When a flu virus spread through the squadron, everyone except Leo would take time off to recoup.

Leo always carried a positive "can-do" attitude. More than anything, he wanted to be a test pilot and astronaut. While we were at Holloman, Leo completed two levels of professional military education—Squadron Officer School and Air Command and Staff College—while finishing a master's degree in engineering. This was a significant accomplishment. It was more typical for an officer to complete only one of the three courses during a single assignment.

Leo was a character, driving around in an old Subaru Brat. You may recall the design—something like a pickup truck with two seats built into the truck bed, facing aft, and handle bars attached to each seat. A really homely vehicle! Leo used to say he liked the caliche mud finish better than the original paint job. I don't think he ever washed the car, not once!

Leo's flight briefings were always entertaining. He'd memorized several lengthy lectures that he'd give to the amusement of us all. He had the ability to repeat rhymes verbatim, time and time again, never missing a beat, always taking the pilots to the point where they were teared up with laughter. If he had a student pilot riding in his back seat, he'd give a briefing about how they were never allowed to speak! There was one exception to the rule. They were allowed to speak if they caught fire and didn't have a checklist available to beat out the flames. At this point they were allowed to scream, "checklist, checklist, checklist," precisely three times. Leo then promised to throw them a checklist with the understanding they would use it to extinguish the flames, and once again be quiet so he could enjoy the remainder of the flight.

Leo lived for the adventure of flying high-performance airplanes. He was a functional check pilot and got to take T-38s up and wring them out after any significant maintenance. I recall one flight where he had lost both engines, got one restarted and headed home. A few minutes later he called to report he'd lost the restarted engine but had managed to get the other engine started. I don't recall how many times this cycle repeated itself but he ended up doing three or four engine restarts before he limped back to Holloman and successfully recovered the aircraft. To him it was the perfect flight—plenty of excitement!

In 1985, I learned I was heading to Colorado to teach Aeronautical Engineering at the Air Force Academy. The application process had taken several months and was very competitive. I still feel fortunate to have had the opportunity. Leo heard about it and decided, very late in the game, he'd like to go to the Academy and teach physics. I shared a concern that the process appeared to be complete for the year. I also asked how he expected the Academy to select someone with degrees in aeronautical and mechanical engineering to teach physics.

Leo wouldn't take no for an answer. He flew to Colorado and told the Academy they couldn't live without him, his selection would be the best they'd ever made, and asked where he'd be sitting. He was selected to teach physics and after the first year was named physics professor of the year! Positive vibrations all the way with a can-do assumption.

Leo's can-do attitude was also apparent when he decided to run the Pike's Peak Marathon. He'd never run long distances before. He said it was simply mind over matter, trained for a couple of months, and he completed the 13.5 mile ascent to the top of Pike's Peak (the maximum allowed for first-time entrants). He wore the wrong shirt the day he ran the marathon, and I can still remember the sight of Leo standing on Pike's Peak, with bloody circles on his white shirt where he'd rubbed his nipples raw. Not a big deal to him; he simply pressed on. Aargh!

Towards the end of our Academy tour I received word I'd be going to fly the F-16 in Japan. Leo decided he wanted to fly in the super secret "black" world of the stealth fighter. The process was pretty well disguised but he ended up flying the F-117 stealth fighter in the Persian Gulf and making the grade of lieutenant colonel.

It was becoming apparent Leo would not achieve his goal of attending the Test Pilot School. He was too senior in rank and the "window" had passed him by. Nonetheless, he wanted to go to Edwards Air Force Base, where the Air Force Test Pilot School is located. Once again he was selected despite not having the typical credentials. He led a team conducting research on advanced concepts in space and missile propulsion technologies. I think he was really in his element at Edwards. He was able to work with academics while at the same time be around the leading edge of experimental flight test.

After Edwards, Leo moved on to Kirtland AFB in New Mexico, where he applied to the astronaut program. My recollection is that, at age 42, he would have been the oldest candidate ever selected. He'd applied to be a mission specialist. When he called to say he'd made the initial cut for the USAF astronaut selection program, he was more excited than I'd ever heard him.

Just a few weeks later I received a call from Leo's wife, Claire, saying Leo had gone on a run, had a massive heart attack and died. She asked if I'd be willing to deliver part of the eulogy. It was one of the more challenging events of my life. Claire said the service would be in a chapel at Kirkland Air Force Base. I pictured a small chapel and prepared my comments in accordance with her suggestion that Leo would have wanted it to include humor. When I arrived at the chapel, I was surprised (and then again not) to find it jam-packed with more than 500 people—Leo's fans.

I struggled to keep my composure standing next to his coffin, looking at the anxious eyes in the chapel. But I found great relief when I started to talk about Leo, his positive attitude, the way he turned difficult situations into fun-filled adventures, and the joy he found in keeping people off balance. The attendees were laughing in short order. I don't think it was the way in which I told the stories so much as it was everyone's recollection of their similar experiences with Leo Broline. His funeral included the first ever F-117 missing-man formation.

Three Leo quotes:

1. "Never eat anything larger than your head."
2. "Why die all tensed up?" (Take life as it comes and not take it too seriously.)
3. "600 knots into a wall of granite."

His attitude about doing one's best right until the very end is something to keep in mind. If you or your troops get down, just remember death is inevitable and what matters is what we do in the remaining time. When Leo went, he was doing 600 knots, driving hard and having fun. I miss him dearly.

We've all heard the quote, "Life is a bitch and then you die." Quit whining and get on with it. Keep things in the proper perspective.

WHY DIE ALL TENSED UP?

I gave a lot of orientation rides in fighters and continue to do so with the L-39 jet I am fortunate to have today as a "boy toy." It is not uncommon for laypersons to have some concern about flying in a fighter. The fact that L-39s come with ejection seats as standard equipment is a bit telling, I suppose. But the reality is the flight will probably be as safe a harbor as any.

My mother used to fear for my life, flying those dangerous jets. I've always shared with her that with my luck I'd go in and resign from the Air Force and then be hit by a bus as I left the building.

In orientation ride situations, I like to remind my passenger of the reality that we all die someday. In fact, for this particular flight, let's just assume we are going to die in a fiery crash. What would you like to do between now and then? Do you want to worry about the inevitable or do you want to enjoy this for all it is worth in the remaining time? Once again, "Why die all tensed up?" In most cases, this causes a chuckle and we get on with the flight.

A flight in a fighter is almost always exciting and rewarding to the orientee (ballast) who rides in the back seat. Why ballast? To a single-seat fighter pilot, anyone occupying space on the airplane is taking the place of additional fuel. Fuel is life when you're flying.

When someone questions whether we should try a new

approach, take a risk with a new product, or call a prospect known to be very difficult and likely to say no or hang up the phone, I like to ask, "What are they going to do? Send us to Minneapolis in the winter months? Wait a minute, we're already here!" Nothing worth going after is easy, so let's accept the fact we'll have to work—pain is part of the equation, life isn't fair, and we won't get everything we dream of—and get on with business.

> **GENERAL (RETIRED) COLIN POWELL:** *Perpetual optimism is a force multiplier. The ripple effect of a leader's enthusiasm and optimism is awesome. So is the impact of cynicism and pessimism. Leaders who whine and blame engender those same behaviors among their colleagues. I am not talking about stoically accepting organizational stupidity and performance incompetence with a "What, me worry?" smile. I am talking about a gung-ho attitude that says, "We can change things here, we can achieve awesome goals, we can be the best." Spare me the grim litany of the "realist," give me the unrealistic aspirations of the optimist any day.*

DEALING WITH NAYSAYERS

> **BUZ BAXTER—BUSINESSMAN, FIGHTER PILOT AND RETIRED MAJOR GENERAL:** *Home runs are hit by people who swing at the ball, so build your team of "swingers."*

Do you remember the "Saturday Night Live" episode where the "Whiners" were at a restaurant and everything was wrong? We've all worked with people who have chosen to go through life with a chip on their shoulder, always being the underdog, never getting the breaks, and choosing to take the negative road. Let me summarize my thoughts by saying, "Get rid of them and right now."

Considering our inability to change people, and the fact these people have a negative effect on the entire team, it is best you accept the situation for what it is, deal with it, and get on with the strategy and tactics without the distraction.

JIM PASCHALL—RANCHER, BUSINESSMAN, FIGHTER PILOT AND RETIRED LIEUTENANT COLONEL: *Sometimes a negative person is such because they have a misunderstanding as to what the goal is. At other times they are like this because the organization is low quality. The first order of business is to determine if such a person has a point. Is there something they do not understand or is something wrong? Take the time to find out. On the other hand, some people are just negative and once that is determined, there is no choice but to escort them out of the area.*

I recently had the opportunity to fly with an intelligent and talented friend who carried over 100 hours of flying time in his logbook and had been a collegiate athlete. As we taxied to take off, he mentioned he was a weak pilot and he was certain I'd be terrified, at least once, during the ride. Believe me, he's not seen a terrifying ride with a student—I'll get back to that story, later.

I suggested we could handle the flight in two ways. I could sit quietly and see if he was going to terrify me, or he could throw this weak pilot story out the window, and we could spend the ride improving his skill set and assuming he was going to become a great pilot with the confidence to move on to more complex flying situations.

He was the product of marginal instruction and, as such, did have some techniques that made for inconsistent process and rough landings. He had been flying with the perception it was his lack of physical and mental skills to blame. Within 45 minutes he was consistently making very smooth landings; his process had improved measurably. It wasn't so much my instructional ability as it was his change in attitude and confidence. He's anxious to go up and learn more and is taking it on directly. He's now chosen to believe he's capable of becoming an outstanding pilot.

I'll reiterate that I believe in taking people and getting results and performance above their expectations. It was certainly a piece of cake to take a talented person, clarify certain process and attitude issues and get above-average results.

I want to go off on a tangent here and share a short story about one of my more challenging students. At the fighter lead-in course, certain instructors were called "red dot" instructors. We flew with students who were having problems, who'd failed some of the rides, and who needed some special attention. If we couldn't turn their performance in a positive direction, then they flew one last evaluation ride and, typically, didn't stay in the fighter business. This was a valid process and of benefit not only to the Air Force but also to the longevity of the pilot and the care of his family.

We had several students from Italy, slotted to become fighter pilots in the Tornado and F-104. I flew with two of them; one was in the top 5 percent of all the students I've flown with, the other was in the bottom 5 percent and on "red dot" status. Let's call the "red dot" student Lieutenant Small. From the moment I met this student I knew he was not going to succeed. He hung his head, mumbled negatively and seemed to live within himself, unaware of the world around him. We called this low-situational awareness. Situational awareness is critical to a fighter pilot. If you aren't aware an enemy plane is 1,000 feet at your six o'clock then you probably won't be expecting the fact you are soon going to be nothing but a red mist!

Lieutenant Small and I first flew together as the fourth airplane in a four-plane formation. We all lined up on the runway, having briefed the procedures for takeoff aborts—what to do if someone ahead of us had a problem and aborted, and how we would avoid each other on the runway in a situation where some of the aircraft had started their takeoff roll and lost an engine. We all ran our engines up to 100 percent RPM, confirmed the engines were good, and #1 started his takeoff roll. Ten seconds later, #2 started to go, followed ten seconds later by #3. Shortly after #3 started the take-off roll, #2 had an engine failure and aborted his takeoff. #3 knew enough to abort his takeoff, since #2 would be blocking his way on the runway. I sat there, taking it all in, pleased we hadn't started the takeoff roll and happy we didn't have to try to stop the many tons of AT-38. The next thing I know, Lieutenant Small released the brakes and called to me, "Afterburners look good, sir." Aargh! Two airplanes with hot brakes are stopped ahead of us, and we're accelerating down the runway with, apparently, the intention of plowing into them at full afterburner. This defines low-situational awareness. Lieutenant Small didn't pass the ride.

Lieutenant Small's last ride in the fighter lead-in course was with me. He barely passed the aforementioned four-ship ride on a flight with another instructor and had to accomplish a formation approach to move to the next phase. A formation approach is one where the lead aircraft flies an approach and lands with the second airplane flying in a precisely defined position "on the wing" through the entire approach and landing. It is critical the wingman fly smoothly, precisely and safely. He needs to stay level with the leader so they touch down simultaneously. He then needs to start his braking before the leader so a safe separation is maintained during deceleration.

We were on a three-mile final approach to the runway on the wing following the leader when our airplane started to climb above the wing of the lead airplane. I asked Lieutenant Small if there was a problem and heard, "Suhr, @###&^$, bree$&**." As we continued our move to the unsafe region above the lead aircraft, I directed my student to put the aircraft back in the proper position as the situation was becoming unsafe. "Siiihr, no #@$%#$$%# can #*&@&$# breathe." I probably let this go on longer than I should have. I knew if I had to take control of the aircraft he would fail the ride, fail the program and be out of fighters for good. Seeing no correction I took the aircraft, executed a missed approach and let the leader land without us. As we flew around the rectangular traffic pattern, I asked the lieutenant to please clearly explain what he was trying to say. I heard him struggle to say, "Sir, no longer can I breathe." I suggested he take off his oxygen mask. He did so and said, "Thank you sir."

This guy was pretty darn clueless. His oxygen hose had come disconnected and an anti-suffocation valve had been activated. It didn't shut off one's ability to breathe; it simply made it more difficult. It served as what we affectionately called "a clue bird." If the clue bird not only craps on your shoulder but also does it several times, you need to take the clue and make a correction. So, the lieutenant had been faced with some decisions. (1) Continue the approach despite the more difficult, but manageable, breathing situation. (2) Share the situation, loosen up the formation for a moment, reconnect the oxygen hose and continue the approach. (3) Panic, and set the formation up for a collision so we could all crash and burn together.

To this day, I think of Lieutenant Small as the most extreme example of poor situational awareness. Years later I met some senior Italian Air Force officers who, having heard I'd instructed at Holloman, asked if I'd ever met the Lieutenant Small. I said yes and they shared that he'd moved to helicopters where he'd totaled one of them. He was sent to "fly a desk" for the rest of his career so he couldn't do any more damage. Takes all kinds. He assumed the negative, was unable to gather up all of the facts and put them into a reasonable order, and he would've died if he'd gone on to a single-seat fighter.

MARK ANDERSON—CONSULTANT, FIGHTER PILOT AND RETIRED LIEUTENANT GENERAL: *I can summarize my thoughts with a one-liner shared by Bill McGoldrick, a consultant who is working with the board of directors of the Air Force Academy's Association of Graduates: "If you think you can, you can; if you think you can't, you're right!*

As an instructor I always did my best to help a student, whatever their natural talents, to make the grade so long as they gave it their best. I can list many an instance where we, as Air Force Academy professors, spent the extra time and effort to help along a student who REALLY wanted to make it. I remember an Air Force Academy football player who came to me and asked for my tutelage, having not passed an aeronautics course on the first go. I spent many an hour; he worked very hard, receiving a relatively high grade. WE got through the course together. In the same semester I recall a naturally talented individual who had an attitude that academics were a waste of time. He was disruptive to the class and ended up not faring as well as the football player. It was all attitudes: positive versus negative, caring versus assumptive and can-do versus don't care.

As leaders we need to be empathetic to our reports, but everything has its limits. If you've spent the time and attempted to convert a negative employee to a real team player, but see no change, set a realistic probationary period. Help as much as is reasonable, and if it doesn't work, help them find some other line of work.

ROGER SCHMITT—BUSINESSMAN, FIGHTER PILOT AND RETIRED COLONEL: *A real benefit in saying "we can get it done" is setting a mindset that there is always hope and we do have a chance to succeed. The opposite stops you dead in the water, kills initiative and gives rise to despair.*

In a recent talk, I shared an example of a senior staff member who, no matter what, would put a negative spin on issues. I asked him to take a more positive look and explained my philosophy as it relates to the need for a positive momentum. I asked him if he wanted us to fail. He said, "Of course not." I asked him if he had chosen to go through life looking only at the dark side. "Of course not." Despite my efforts, he did not change. I'd set the bar at a certain height, and he'd suggest it was too high. We'd compromise and lower the bar a bit, and he'd come back and say he thought it was unrealistic. I'd ask him where, specifically, we should set the bar, and he wouldn't have an answer. Milquetoast! Noncommittal! He'd chosen the dark side, liked to be miserable and wanted everyone else to be miserable. He was not a valuable team member. I suggested he might be happier outside of our company, and I think he is. I guess he found a place where they appreciate his bringing that negative perspective to the table. He found a place where they find value in being paranoid about the future. Life is short, and I choose to be positive about it. Others are free to leave, and right now.

DAVID FISHER—BUSINESSMAN, FINANCIAL CONSULTANT AND ENTREPRENEUR: *I would much rather hire an employee who has the right work ethic and a positive, "can-do" outlook—even though they may be lacking in specific knowledge or experience—than an employee who has the perfect résumé. An enthusiastic, always positive and hard-working employee is contagious. Fellow workers will need to step up or risk being left behind. An employee with a sour attitude is bad yeast.*

As it relates to positive thinking:
- Momentum and the positive motivation model.
- Why die all tensed up?
- Dealing with naysayers.

GIVING CREDIT

8

> *"The way to get things done is not to mind*
> *who gets the credit for doing them."*
> **Benjamin Jowett**

In this second chapter on team we'll discuss:

- Giving credit where credit is due.
- Rarely see milestones met by the efforts of a single person.
- Be prepared to accept responsibility when things don't go well.

GIVING CREDIT WHERE CREDIT IS DUE

> *"Tact is the art of convincing people that*
> *they know more than you do."*
> **Raymond Mortimer,**
> ***1895–1980***

What goes around comes around. The more credit you can give away to those truly

Giving Credit

Milestones

Accept Responsibility

deserving, the more effective you'll be as a leader. I've always liked the suggestion a leader needs to "catch someone doing something right." In our interactions with direct reports and others, we need to solicit feedback about activities and progress; sort out parts that have made a difference to the team, mission and atmosphere; and reinforce it all with recognition.

ROGER SCHMITT—BUSINESSMAN, FIGHTER PILOT AND RETIRED COLONEL: *I believe in always giving credit where it is due, but don't go overboard lavishing praise for standard performance or you will end up establishing a lower standard. If you give away praise for mediocre performance, then when you really want to credit someone or the group, it will have a lesser, diluted impact. I've seen this happen numerous times. It also becomes a problem during review time when people have unrealistic expectations based on previous, superficial and perhaps flowery remarks made by the reviewer.*

Candid, objective and timely feedback is key to moving your organization down a path of continuous improvement. People are naturally motivated to contribute and add value. Many a time I've seen people overmanaged, underappreciated and reinforced in a negative fashion. How can you expect them to make contributions commensurate with their potential?

DR. SANDRA DAVIS—CORPORATE EXECUTIVE, AUTHOR AND PSYCHOLOGIST: *I want to go back to one thing on recognition. When we started the business, the person I founded the business with had been in the military. When we talked about the values of the organization we wanted to create, one of the things he said to me was, "Officers eat last." He was very clear about that. While I've never been in the military, that statement has always made sense to me. That is, it is our job as leaders* *to pay attention to the needs of the people in the organization first and our own needs last.*

From the first day of business we have always shared profits with the entire staff. No matter what job you have here, if the whole team creates a profitable year, everyone shares in that profit. So if you happen to be the receptionist, you might go home with a 20 percent bonus for the year because the firm did phenomenally well. I truly believe if we all create something really terrific, then we all share in the rewards. Part of our rewards and recognition here is sharing in the profits of the company. And that will always be a tenet for me.

Let me start with an example of how *not* to lead a team. The single worst reporting situation I experienced as an Air Force officer was imbedded in the single best assignment I had as a pilot. I absolutely loved the environment, atmosphere, mission and quality of personnel at Holloman Air Force Base, New Mexico. However, for a short time I worked for a senior officer who took all the credit; ruled through fear, sarcasm and ridicule; and significantly decreased overall effectiveness despite the high quality found in his staff. This officer had a huge ego with an enormous need for personal recognition, and he figured his team was there to make him look good. As a flight examiner, he intimidated the examinees. They knew he needed to be managed very carefully by not bruising his ego, and somehow finding a way to make him feel even better about himself. No one liked the guy or sincerely supported him, and he had a negative effect on our productivity.

During that time I spent about a month rewriting a flying regulation that needed to be approved by the general overseeing the Air Force base. My boss took the opportunity to take my work and present it to the general as his own. He wanted the recognition—although he could have sent me with the work I'd completed to not only give me the ownership and responsibility, but to also get me some exposure with the person ultimately responsible for promotions. The document had come back with two very small changes that I quickly made on my word processor. The corrections required were both extremely minor (a comma changed to a period and *it* changed to *them*). When this was complete, knowing we had only until the end of the day to get the corrected version approved, I delivered it to the general's assistant.

When I returned to my office, the "boss from hell" had returned from flying and was waiting and asked to see the corrected document. I said I'd already made the minor changes and returned the document. He was furious and directed me to return to the general's office, recover the document and deliver it to his desk. When I did so, he didn't read it. He simply slapped the document with his hand and said, "In the future I want to see everything that goes out of this office, and nothing is delivered to the general's office without my specific approval." He didn't even look at the document. I took it back, the general's assistant did some eye rolling, and I headed back for my next "lashing."

I can't think of a single instance where we received positive reinforcement from this officer. I can think of a dozen times where he took credit for work done by others. Each experience was a "significant emotional event" in a negative way for the team. We survived it but it could have been much, much more pleasant and productive. Moreover, many of us carry this sort of stress home. We don't sleep as well, we don't care about exercise, we look for ways to avoid our work, and we have an overall depleted, negative attitude. In the long run, the self-centered leader is recognized as such by their management and, once again, "what goes around comes around." This all ties back to creating a positive work atmosphere; unfortunately we're going to run into people like the "boss from hell" who don't see the big picture. What's needed is humility.

BUZ BAXTER—BUSINESSMAN, FIGHTER PILOT AND RETIRED MAJOR GENERAL: *Humility is next to godliness. When everything is going smoothly, it's a piece of cake to hear all the nice things being said and accept the praise with an "Aw, shucks." If I were a weatherman, I would never accept, "Thanks for the nice day ... "—first, I wouldn't deserve it because I didn't make it; and second, I wouldn't want to have to explain away the tornado that might blow in tomorrow.*

I deal with self-centered employees directly and expeditiously. I once took a profiling test before joining a large corporation. Afterwards, the psychologist noted that political maneuvering and positioning were at the absolute bottom of my "tolerable traits" list. It doesn't help our strategy if team members are worried about their next job, trying to look better than their peers, or spending precious time aligning themselves for personal gain. I think less of people who spend time strategically positioning themselves and giving attention to workplace politics. There is a difference between this undesirable focus on self and the desirable focus on doing one's own best work for the team. When you take the opportunity to demonstrate and communicate the value of this trait to your employees, some may come around.

DR. SANDRA DAVIS—CORPORATE EXECUTIVE, AUTHOR AND PSYCHOLOGIST: *I am a firm believer in management by wandering around and noticing the small things someone has done in a particular day or week and commenting about it. We once did a recognition and rewards study with employees in a state department. In that study we were trying to find out what people wanted by way of recognition and reward. The department wanted a new recognition and reward system in place. They wanted to know whether people* *wanted plaques or recognition in the newsletter. By far and away the number one thing people wanted was positive feedback from their manager about what they did well. When we asked about a time when you felt really good about the recognition you received, we heard things like, "well, it was the letter someone sent me about this." Or, it was, "my boss's boss dropped in and said 'I saw what you did and that was fabulous work. You're the kind of person we need.'" Those were the messages that really mattered to people.*

That being said, people like to be recognized in different ways. Some people really do like to see their picture in a newsletter. Some hate to see their picture on the company bulletin board. Some would love to have a new picture for their new wall and others might like to be sent to a professional conference. If you want to know what people want for recognition and reward, it's really simple. Ask. Because each person is motivated so differently, don't assume that if you have wandered up and down the hall, said hello to everyone and patted them on the back, they must all feel recognized and rewarded. Guess again. You won't be right or you won't be as effective as you could be unless you find out what's really important to people. Personally, I know to say the words, and I know the things people like and want, but I'm still not as good at this as I could be.

Have you ever seen something called The Languages of Appreciation? In his book, Inspire, Persuade, Lead: Communication Secrets of Excellent Leaders, *Paul Batz says that he has people go through five different ways in which appreciation can be shown and describe which is their preference. The five languages of appreciation are words of encouragement, acts of service, gift giving, quality time and physical touch and closeness. People really do put these in a different order for themselves. Paul uses an example in his book of a person who gave his wife wonderful jewelry every Christmas. He wondered why she seldom wore it. He had worked very hard in finding the perfect gift. One day he discovered she had a stack of all the cards he'd given her along with the jewelry in the past. He wondered why she had not worn the jewelry often but still had all the cards. She said, "These cards and the words you wrote mean more to me than any gift of jewelry."*

As an employee you should know your job, do the work, and give it your best. The system will take care of the personal recognition, promotions and rewards. A friend of mine often asks, "Who is going to pick up the shovel and do the work?" If someone on your team—manager or otherwise—is working hard and passing as much credit as possible to teammates, they are precisely the type of person you want. Giving due credit helps create the positive atmosphere we will discuss at length later on.

RARELY SEE MILESTONES MET BY THE EFFORTS OF A SINGLE PERSON

BUZ BAXTER—BUSINESSMAN, FIGHTER PILOT AND RETIRED MAJOR GENERAL: *The fact of the matter is that almost nothing done today is the product of one person; thus no one person should seek or accept praise for a deed without publicly acknowledging all others who participated in the successful venture.*

As dull as the laundry-list acceptance speech may seem to the Academy Award viewer, it is a model of positive leadership. Great leaders take the time to recognize all components of a successful solution. They recognize that the "support component" of a successful venture needs to be acknowledged.

JIM PASCHALL—RANCHER, BUSINESSMAN, FIGHTER PILOT AND RETIRED LIEUTENANT COLONEL: *There is no better way to get a group pumped than being able to convince them that "they did it." Usually there is one person who stays in the background unrecognized by the group while all the time pulling a load. Singling out that person oftentimes pays great dividends.*

We used to have "turkey shoots" where pilots would compete in air-to-ground weapons delivery. It was an opportunity to compete squadron to squadron and pilot to pilot in events including bomb-dropping accuracy, strafing accuracy and other events like low-level navigation and time-on-target proficiencies. Over the years, I've won some awards in these activities and was always eager to compete with my compadres. However, my winning was ultimately dependent on the support team.

One specific example is flying the AT-38 trainer we used at the Lead-In-Fighter Training course. The airplane needed to be well maintained, properly configured and ready to go on time if one had any hope of winning the event. Having the airplane fueled, the armament properly loaded and the weapons in alignment was critical.

The AT-38 had a very crude aiming device for strafe. The SU-11 mini-gun was a 7.62mm Gattling gun mounted on the centerline of the aircraft belly. The strafe target is only a few feet across, the firing range is thousands of feet, and an alignment error of one degree at one mile is 100 feet of error—more than enough to eliminate a pilot from the competition. So, if we were fortunate enough to know which airplane we'd be flying and which ground crew was responsible for it, we could make quite a difference by showing support to the ground crew and motivating them to be part of a winning combination. Their extra effort made all the difference. Recognition inspired going the extra mile, and buying-in to the competition made for a winning team.

So many team members, military or corporate, are not recognized for their work and are not encouraged. They may not even be aware of the mission. We can't expect them to do the best job possible without high levels of communication and recognition for work well done. By letting them know you consider them part of the team, and that they can make or break the effort, you are empowering them to make a difference. As a support team member, it would be difficult to imagine spending the extra time or effort to make an organization (or even a strafe mission) more successful if I don't understand the significance or think my efforts are appreciated. Ignoring this concept leads to the all-too-common scenario of average people doing average work.

While flying the AT-38 in New Mexico, I worked with a crew chief by the name of Staff Sergeant Patterson. Sergeant Patterson's attitude and efforts far surpassed the average support team member. I recall visiting him one Saturday in a maintenance hanger where he was polishing the airplane to a brilliant shine. The pitot tube, normally a dull pewter-like finish, looked like chrome. I asked where he'd found it, thinking the chrome tube might be a special addition since we'd picked up some of the former Air Force Thunderbird aircraft. He said it took hours of polishing, no tricks, no shortcut, just hard work and a desire to be the best at his job.

The shine didn't make much of a difference to aircraft performance, bombing accuracy or our ability to instruct students. Nonetheless, he had such a pride in his work he wanted to go the extra mile to make the airplane appear to be the finest in the fleet. His uniform was always pressed; his hair was always perfect; his airplane, tail number 550, was always immaculate. He had a profound effect on me as well. When I flew the airplane, I walked towards it a bit differently, knowing Sergeant Patterson had put the effort forth. I flew a bit better, and I won a few more events. Let me tell you though, one of the reasons Sergeant Patterson worked hard and made a difference was because I went out of my way, as I'm sure other pilots did, to let him know his contribution was significant. He never asked for praise, but ended up being promoted and named the "Crew Chief of the Year" out of a large field of contenders. I guarantee he worked even harder to make a difference after the recognition.

Sometimes, despite our best efforts, there are acts of God that come into play. Let me share the unfortunate details of AT-38 #550. Sergeant Patterson and I were chosen to fly the airplane to Las Vegas for what was then called the NATO Generals' Meet. We put the aircraft on "static display" for the air show. I answered questions while he did his usual exemplary job keeping the airplane in showroom condition. On our return flight we felt a slight vibration at high airspeeds. After landing we walked around the airplane but couldn't find any visible clues as to where the vibration came from, so we wrote up our concerns in the aircraft logbook. The airplane was taken off the flying schedule for an engine replacement the following week.

When this happens a pilot is asked to do a "functional check flight" on the airplane before it is allowed back on the flight line for the sake of instructional flights. A squadron pilot was asked to make the check flight. At high speed over the lava flows of the White Sands Missile Range, the tail of the airplane broke off, the airplane went out of control, and the pilot had to eject at around 500 knots, a fatally dangerous speed. He suffered multiple dislocations and other serious injuries. The pilot was very fortunate that the winds were low that day since he was unable to move his arms or to disconnect his parachute after landing near the lava flow. He spent quite a bit of time in the hospital before being released to head out and fly fighters again. That was, of course, the last flight for tail number 550. I've wondered what would have happened if the tail had come off the airplane as we were flying back from Las Vegas over the Rocky Mountains. Sergeant Patterson never could have known there was a weak bearing in the tail of 550. He was assigned another aircraft, which, in short order was the best looking rig on the ramp.

When we give away the credit, we can also give away some of the responsibility. As our leadership responsibilities expand, it becomes critical that we delegate our duties and become more of a conductor. Many times a leader grows from a situation where they were responsible for all of the details associated with a certain job. It is difficult to make the leap from owning all of the details to empowering our reports to worry about them. It is critical senior leadership stay far enough away from the day-to-day operation to keep perspective at a higher level. Someone needs to continue to provide the clarity in vision and strategy discussed in previous chapters.

SAM WESTBROOK—CONSULTANT, BUSINESSMAN, FIGHTER PILOT AND RETIRED BRIGADIER GENERAL: *Try and make yourself dispensable rather than indispensable, so the organization will continue to function effectively if you walk out in front of a delivery truck tomorrow. Give people the tools they need to do the job, and then stand back and applaud when they succeed. Not everybody gets from point A to point B the same way. Set the parameters that need to be met and turn them loose. One might even learn a few tricks.*

In sales organizations it is typical to see the top salesperson get colorful awards, a big bonus, and the most recognition. The high performance salespeople I've managed are hard-driving, outgoing individuals who live for the challenge of starting from scratch every month and making their living one sale at a time. At quite a number of businesses, salespeople are commission-only. If they don't sell, they don't eat!

DAVID FISHER—BUSINESSMAN, FINANCIAL CONSULTANT AND ENTREPRENEUR: *Let other people take the credit, or better, give other people the credit. Ronald Reagan is the shining example of this, and his manage-*

ment style as president is a great example. Jack Welch was quick to point out he was surrounded by great managers, who largely should be given credit for the success of the organization.

As a sales manager it is important to stroke the salespeople in a manner that motivates the proper behaviors, keeps them making the calls, attending the seminars and building relationships. However, we must not lose sight of the fact the effectiveness of our sales force is directly dependent on all of the support areas. A sales call requires collateral materials, presentations, Web site demonstrations, referrals and a positive operational history. Set expectations, reward where appropriate and don't praise only the quarterback.

ACCEPT RESPONSIBILITY
WHEN THINGS DON'T GO WELL

"If you take all the credit, you must take all the blame!"
General Buz Baxter

A great leader takes responsibility when things go awry. Remember my comments about sitting for the Eagle Scout examination? It turns out that taking responsibility for the fact I didn't have an answer was precisely what the board wanted to see. If ever you find yourself or your team in trouble, it is best to take full responsibility. Whether you were in a position to control the situation will come out in the wash. The way you handle these scenarios has a huge impact on how your team perceives you and how members support each other. The default should be that your people did the right thing, and whatever happened is ultimately your responsibility.

"To develop into a great leader one must have the desire to lead, the ability to be a decision maker and the willingness to accept responsibility."
Steven H. Wheeler

Let me give another example of the negative effect of not accepting responsibility or not understanding the concept of taking ownership can have on a team. I once worked on an outstanding team of fighter pilots where the person in charge was "leadership challenged"—a huge demotivator for a team. The top positions should go to the top performers. As a friend always says, "Lead or get out of the way." This guy was in the way, and big time! I'll once again show my intolerance for those who are more concerned with perception than getting the job done. This particular example illustrates not only a reluctance to accept responsibility but the need for at least a basic level of technical competence in the person expected to lead from the front.

When I showed up (as one of the top five ranking officers in the squadron), I was told if I wanted feedback from the commander, I should stop by the bar— great start! This guy was a piece of work. He was not competent in the F-16, and one day landed the airplane far too fast. He should have done a missed approach, come around again and landed at the proper airspeed. Instead, he used the brakes to stop the airplane. So what? We all use the brakes to stop the airplane. Well, he was going so fast the brakes melted and fused together.

Big mistake. He could have shared with the pilots "how not to land an F-16." Instead, he called the maintenance folks and asked them to hurry the airplane into a hanger and get it fixed before the word got out he'd messed up his landing. The maintenance crews were sharing the story with everyone. The pilots knew about it immediately, and yet the commander never shared it with the squadron nor admitted to having been involved in the aircraft incident. It was a classic attempt to cover up an issue he could have shared in a way that could have actually generated respect for the commander and imparted wisdom as well.

At the same assignment, with the same commander, a senior flight commander nearly "bought the farm" on a night mission with bad weather where he experienced vertigo in the F-16. The F-16 canopy is curved in such a way that it can be disorienting at night due to the reflection of the cockpit gages on the canopy. My friend, a fairly senior pilot in the squadron with thousands of hours of fighter experience, lost his situational awareness in the clouds at night in the single-seat fighter. He found himself flying straight up, recognized the decreasing airspeed and increasing altitude, and lit the afterburner to avoid departing "controlled flight." In this situation any airplane, other than one comparable in performance to the F-16, would have forced the pilot to eject.

The pilot got on top of the clouds, reoriented himself and made a successful recovery to the airbase where he went immediately to the men's room and cleaned out his shorts. He had scared himself and recognized that as a senior pilot this could happen to anyone, especially younger pilots. He went into the commander, 'fessed up and asked to have the opportunity to share this with the other squadron pilots. Disapproved! The commander didn't want this highlighted to his bosses for fear he would be held responsible. Instead, he went around the squadron discrediting the flying ability of this major and removed him from his position as a flight commander in the squadron.

Don't punish your team for taking responsibility for things that go wrong. If they are willing to do this, it says a lot about their self-confidence, integrity and focus on the team's long-term success.

At the military academies, it is typical to train the cadets to say "No excuse, sir." If a mistake is made, the proper action is to take responsibility, not to waffle about how it happened, why it happened, and why you are not at fault. Accept responsibility.

Think about that for a minute. If you make a mistake, walk into your boss's office and fully disclose the mistake, what are they going to say? I believe you've disarmed their desire to implement a significant consequence. In fact, a strong leader will already be looking for ways to help you out of a bad situation, so long as your heart was in the right place. Personally, I deliver bad news to my bosses as quickly and accurately as possible.

If my sales team isn't going to make a quota, I want my superiors to know about it as early as possible. It allows me to move on to correcting the deficiency, to focus on the next sales goal and NOT spend my time worrying about the consequence of one bad month. If there is bad news I like to say, "This isn't even going to matter in five years." Let's take responsibility, learn from our mistakes, let the water pass under the bridge, empower the team to keep on truckin', and keep the distraction to a minimum. Get back to working in the present!

Then-Colonel Sam Westbrook was our Deputy Commander for Operations (DO) at RAF Upper Heyford, England. As I previously mentioned, he is one of the greatest leaders I've worked for, and I continue to solicit his sage advice.

The DO was responsible for flying operations at Upper Heyford. Three squadrons of pilots and weapons systems operators (WSOs) that flew the F-111 fighter-bombers reported to him. The F-111 was complex, the flying environment was dangerous because of the low altitudes at which we'd operate, and the weather in England was typically awful. Just before I arrived, an airplane had crashed, killing the two crew members. In my first few months we lost two more airplanes, one piloted by a very close friend. Another—an airplane I was supposed to fly that day—had a mechanical failure and killed both the pilot and WSO. It felt about as close to a wartime assignment as possible in peacetime.

Colonel Westbrook put together a monthly meeting for the air crews called the "DO Dialogue." During that time, selected air crews were expected to stand in front of their peers, share the mistakes they'd made and provide a constructive summary for the sake of continuous improvement. The environment was one where mistakes were expected to happen and lessons were expected to be learned. Don't get me wrong, although this was a very positive learning environment, it did not allow for things like the buzzing of aunts in Scotland. Punishment was an option for those who sought it!

During the assignment, a young lieutenant found himself disoriented at night over England, while looking for a refueling tanker. He flew through some altitude restrictions and nearly hit the refueling tanker. The tanker co-pilot commented that he saw the afterburner flames from the F-111 hit the windscreen of the tanker. It was a close call. All of the tanker crew members as well as the F-111 crew members could have perished. The pilot shared the events that led up to the near-miss at DO Dialogue, got additional training for disorientation and we all became better pilots for the lessons learned. Accept responsibility, share the facts of the matter, and move on to your next challenge.

I'll go on one more tangent to share an experience that put me closer to ejecting from a fighter than I've ever experienced. And, yes, I got to share this one at DO Dialogue.

Mike Graham, a great WSO, and I were flying a simulated low-altitude attack in Northern England. This was a situation where we flew a few hundred feet above the ground, somewhere around 500 knots, so the WSO could fine-tune his radar bombing skill set. The weather was somewhat typical for England—low clouds, light rain and marginal visibility. We were just getting into the final portion of this particular attack sequence when we took a lightning strike on the nose of the F-111.

The airplane's pitot-static system was destroyed by the pressure pulse, the electrical system took a jolt that shut down the flight control computers, and the shock wave generated by the strike compressor stalled both of our engines. We followed the standard procedure, pulled the nose up 20 degrees, called out on the radio to report our dilemma and initiated engine restart procedures. The aircraft instrumentation was limited. We had the inertial navigation system groundspeed, the attitude indicators, and the altimeter and radios. Another problem was our climb had put us in the clouds, complicating our situation.

There were no outside references, just checklists and procedures as we worked through our situation. Mike had raised the ejection handles and was ready to squeeze the handle that would have initiated the ejection sequence. As it turns out we did not eject. The entire sequence from lightning strike to making the decision to not eject from the multimillion dollar airplane was around 20 seconds.

Long story short, we got an engine started, climbed above the clouds and joined up with another F-111 crew who took us home to RAF Upper Heyford. It was an exciting experience for a 25-year-old. I remember being met by then-Colonel Tony McPeak. He climbed up the aircraft ladder, congratulated us on recovering the airplane and suggested we get out. I remember having been cool as ice throughout the event and then not having the strength in my knees to deplane.

In summary:
- Giving credit where credit is due.
- Rarely see milestones met by the efforts of a single person.
- Be prepared to accept responsibility when things don't go well.

9

GENERATING ENTHUSIASM

In this chapter we'll discuss:

- Sprints and long drives.
- Input from everyone.
- Walk around management.
- Caring for your people.

"In things pertaining to enthusiasm, no man is sane who does not know how to be insane on proper occasions."
Henry Ward Beecher,
1813–1887

SPRINTS AND LONG DRIVES

I know I'm enjoying my work if I wake up early, rush through my shower and dash to the office. I also know I really enjoy taking what may appear to be a monumental project and breaking it into smaller sprints. As people like to say, "you need to eat an elephant—one bite at a time."

We've already discussed the importance of having a team vision and strategy for long-term success. For me as the CEO, the vision is something I've helped develop and something I am personally responsible for reaching. For those who are not on the senior staff, it may be difficult to get excited about the corporation's lofty vision. Therefore, it is important we create a subset of sprints that get us to the vision one sprint at a time.

JEAN SCHLEMMER—CORPORATE EXECUTIVE: *I know we talk a lot about motivating people. I actually don't know how much you can motivate people. I think that's very much an inner thing. I think you can inspire people, and I certainly think you can de-motivate them.*

My own group and I believe there are a couple of key components to "growing people." You need to create the proper environment, an atmosphere in which they can grow. It has to do with providing opportunities, doing some risk taking and being committed to the whole concept of growth. But probably even more important, you have to take the time to know your people. And that comes, I think, in part by hiring right in the first place. You know, hire slowly, and fire quickly. Know how they're wired, know their strengths. Otherwise you can spend an awful lot of time trying to manage and motivate them.

If the company vision is to become number one in customer service, we need to break that into division-specific action items for the team. The Web site people need to make their agreed-upon site improvements by a certain date. The head of IT needs to drive his team to that goal, create an enthusiasm and tie it to recognition and reward. Bonuses should be aligned with specific, measurable, attainable, reasonable and timely goals. Similarly, the head of customer service needs to decide what training, outgoing call activity and coaching needs to take place by a certain date to improve their performance.

DR. SANDRA DAVIS—CORPORATE EXECUTIVE, AUTHOR AND PSYCHOLOGIST: *People generate enthusiasm in so many different ways. There is not a single formula for it. But there is magic in someone who can come in and energize a group. Having someone in the organization with the ability to do that is terrific. If the leader doesn't have it, bring in someone who does and be clear about what you want that person to do. People do a lot of different things to generate enthusiasm. Customer Research Inc. had a bell ringer award when they were really focusing in on sales and wanted to get everyone conscious about sales. They had a bell that was rung down in the lobby that let everyone know, "Guess what? We just scored another one." And then it would start a buzz around the organization and people felt the momentum building.*

Customer Research Inc. has also done some interesting things related to both goal setting and enthusiasm. For example, one year as they set their revenue targets, they also told their people they'd take everyone to San Francisco for a two-day weekend "if we reach such and such a target." And literally, they took everyone in the company. It didn't matter when you started, you went. They put a map up on the wall and tracked sales goals as if they were starting in New York. Everyone could follow the route to see how close they were to getting to San Francisco. They did the same thing when the goal was to get to London. In both cases they made the goal. That builds enthusiasm because it's something really tangible. It's real. People need things that are real to build enthusiasm. I think leaders need to use the "emotion" words when talking with people about what we're doing. "This is terrific, I'm really pleased. I can't believe what a fabu-

lous job you all did." That kind of language and support builds enthusiasm as well.

People love to see they're doing things together, knowing the goals were accomplished together. Despite the fact there will be some who want to be stars—and you want to give the superstars some chance to be stars—people also love to be able to say we all did this together. It builds a lot of enthusiasm. I heard about a Pizza Hut manager who has everyone run together in the morning. I will bet that worked because it drove home the point that it is about all of us together. Maybe it worked so well because we know people need to be healthy in order to perform well. Maybe the run was a better stress reliever than an enthusiasm builder. Who knows? We all have to find what works for us.

If you came to my business first thing in the morning you won't find the morning songs or pep rallies that some organizations do. That wouldn't pass the snicker or smell test here. It might some places. You've got to figure out what's going to pass the "snicker meter" for your own organization, so people aren't thinking, "I can't believe what the boss wants us to do this time."

When I was given the task of lowering the monthly cash burn rate for one company, I knew I couldn't do it by myself. I needed to have every employee thinking about expense reduction. I used a technique learned in the Air Force. If we hit our monthly goals, then the last weekend of the month became a three-day weekend for everyone. Using that technique, I posted our current burn rate, the goal for six months down the road and a straight line of our monthly cash burn target.

We needed to decrease spending from $1.2 million to $650,000 per month over six months. When the short- and long-term goals were communicated, the incentive put in place, and the enthusiasm for the goals generated, the team went to work. The power of the many minds was unleashed!

Admin, HR, legal, finance, marketing, sales and IT all scrubbed their budgets and found ways to reduce cost. We not only hit our goals, we exceeded them in a significant manner. In the first month alone we dropped our expenditures by about 20 percent. We made our remaining goals every month and found we could run effectively, and much more efficiently, at a monthly burn rate of around $550,000. My job was not to dig through financials and find cost savings myself, but rather to reinforce the efforts being made by every individual in the company—to catch them doing something right!

Total Economic Burn Rate

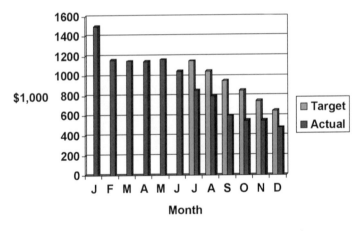

Month

Perhaps the largest win, from this sprint, was the empowerment of the individuals and their newfound understanding of the ability they have to really make a difference.

SAM WESTBROOK—CONSULTANT, BUSINESSMAN, FIGHTER PILOT AND RETIRED BRIGADIER GENERAL:
I particularly like using sprints and longer drives in combination. The thing I found that got people really excited

was when we were able to set up a system that convinced people their ideas about how to do the job better would be welcomed (even demanded), fairly and rapidly evaluated and then implemented. Regular visits from higher ranking people to the places where the work is actually being done is also a great morale booster—if the visitor takes the time to be interested in and communicate with the work force. Such visits also serve an accountability function; since people are less apt to be goofing off or goofing up if they know an unannounced visit is a possibility.

INPUT FROM EVERYONE

One tried-and-true method for determining if you have a motivated and enthusiastic group is to gather everyone in a conference room and run them through a team challenge and problem-solving exercise. If you get input only from the senior staff with no dialogue at all from the rest of the team, there is room for improvement. Whenever I am given responsibility for a new area, staff or team, I like to make it clear I cannot run the organization alone.

Make sure your direct reports know you aren't there to tell them what to do. You are going to empower them to run their organizations and hold them accountable for what they claim they'll do. The reason we have a team is to take advantage of the collective minds for problem solving. There is no doubt that a group of people, motivated to provide input, is more likely to think through alternatives and consequences than a single decision maker. If they can't come to the table with new ideas, constructive feedback and a willingness to make a difference, they aren't a fit.

Without exception, I always find at least one individual who quietly attends the meetings and doesn't take part in the activities. If you've ever spent time in a think-tank atmosphere, you know it is critical for every member to share thoughts if you want to have creative output. You, the leader, need to create an atmosphere that encourages input, fosters constructive dialogue and reinforces the input of all team members, no matter how bizarre the ideas may seem at the time. If you can do this, you'll find the organization much more productive, and you'll generate an enthusiasm among the team that's otherwise dormant.

I look around the group and try to keep an eye on those team members known for sitting quietly while the rest of the group discusses possible solutions. If I pick up on any reaction to a specific discussion, I turn to that person and ask them to share their thoughts with the group. I'm very careful to not embarrass a team member who doesn't like speaking out, but at the same time I reinforce any input they offer.

No such thing as a stupid question! I once had a team meeting for our entire company where I provided my outlook for the next year. At the end of the presentation I asked if there were any questions or comments. After several other comments, a receptionist raised her hand and asked a question about reviews and raises. She prefaced her question with, "I know this is probably a stupid question, but ... "

We were reducing expenses and fighting for our survival, and most had recognized we would have to freeze salaries and bonuses until we knew the company would remain viable. The receptionist should have known this since every employee had received written notice plus I had one-on-one meetings with everyone— including her. Nonetheless, it was critical to treat her with grace and to reinforce her input to the conversation.

I thanked her for the question and spent a couple of minutes talking about our situation, my desire to get us back to business as usual, and I encouraged her to continue to ask any questions she might have. Afterwards several individuals made negative comments to me about this woman's question. To me it was a good sign the environment had created enough confidence so the receptionist would ask a question in front of the entire company. She felt empowered to do so and, afterward, carried an enthusiasm for her job that was apparent. I took the opportunity to provide feedback to the people making negative comments and coached them on the value of input and empowerment across the entire team. They picked up on my style and my lack of support for their criticism, and there were no repeat performances.

DAVID FISHER—BUSINESSMAN, FINANCIAL CONSULTANT AND ENTREPRENEUR: *My firm runs small sales-oriented contests from time to time. Rewards are given to the employee with the greatest number of new accounts, most new assets, etc. At first I thought they were trivial, but the truth is, I have been highly motivated by them. The rewards are no big deal and definitely not worth the time and work involved—dinner for two at a local restaurant, a gift certificate at the local mall, that sort of thing. What motivates is at the end of the contest; the results are given to everyone in the office. The opportunity to show you can outperform your peers (and get a free dinner to boot . . .) is a big motivator.*

If you want your team to be enthusiastic about the mission, they need to be part of the consequence as well. On the negative side, if the company fails, everyone loses their jobs. Don't need to do a lot of homework to figure that one out. On the positive side, I believe in giving ownership in the company to as many employees as possible. It isn't really the size of the option grants (a stock ownership option) so much as having a stake.

I've found the process of educating those who haven't had options in the past is worthwhile. Explaining that one's every action adds or subtracts from the company worth, as well as the ultimate value of the option grant, is a motivator. Many people have never had a job where they make the connection between their "value add" and the company's success. Nor have they ever been tied financially to the company's success.

The option grants tie back to recognition and the point that no matter how small, it matters. Everyone is motivated differently; some may not care about the financial rewards as much as being in the spotlight. So how do you find out what motivates your people? You ask them. If Bill prefers some time off to spend with his family, then tie his performance to a vacation day bonus. If Jane wants nothing but financial reward, so be it!

No matter how well you understand these concepts, it isn't going to be as effective if you can't push it down through your organizational structure. About the best I can do is get my senior staff to understand, by example, the benefits outlined in this chapter (and the book as a whole). You need to be a coach to your senior staff. They need to be coaches to their management staff. If everyone understands the concepts we're talking about, right down to the copy clerk in one of your offices, then we're talking about an effective organization.

BUZ BAXTER—BUSINESSMAN, FIGHTER PILOT AND RETIRED MAJOR GENERAL: *We all know the distinctions between coach, quarterback and cheerleader. The true leader is a little bit of all of these and encourages and develops enthusiasm by the care he demonstrates for his people, his devotion to mission, sincerity of purpose, dedication to principle, caution in the face of risk, courage in the face of danger, plus his regular participation in decisions, activities . . . and the tolerance of isolated, inconsequential, undesirable, sometimes unsavory events. He accepts blame for his own errors and expects his immediate staff to work for their subordinates while supporting him. He is not stingy with his praise for performance, but he is selective in his pronouncement of it, lest it loses it value. ENTHUSIASM is best generated by example.*

ROGER SCHMITT—BUSINESSMAN, FIGHTER PILOT AND RETIRED COLONEL: *It's imperative everyone feels part of the team and the organization provides a satisfying environment for its people. The interest of employees is best served when they are satisfied with what they receive, in return for their efforts. It's also important that leadership understands what really motivates people— and it's not always money.*

WALK AROUND MANAGEMENT

I recall a "turkey shoot" while I was stationed at RAF Upper Heyford, England. That was an F-111 sortie generation and bombing accuracy competition between three squadrons. We were towards the end of the competition and had just one more flight to get off the ground and drop a single practice bomb on Wainfleet range, on the East Coast of England.

As I walked up to the airplane, having just landed from another flight, the maintenance people were walking around the belly of the airplane where a piece of aluminum had come off. We were all very frustrated at the thought we wouldn't be able to make the flight, drop the bomb and win the competition.

Right in the middle of the fray was Lieutenant Colonel Bob Riddick, our squadron commander. He surveyed the damage from underneath the airplane, and then walked up to the flight crew and the maintenance supervisor. He said it was up to us, but it looked pretty grim. We were very tight on getting the damage fixed and making it to the bombing range in the remaining time, but it was up to us to decide if we wanted to take a shot at getting the flight off and winning the competition.

Well, there was no question! The maintenance folks quickly took off the damaged part while my weapons system operator and I climbed into the jet and did all of our preflight checks. The minute the part was fixed, the other maintenance team members gave us a thumbs up to start. Everything went like clockwork, and we flew directly to the bombing range and dropped the bomb to win the competition.

This would not have happened if Bob Riddick hadn't been right there, offering encouragement and empowering us to make the decision. He could have stood around and been directive, but would not have started the fires in all of us that drove us to get it done, no matter what. He was always that way: present and offering support whenever we turned around, yet empowering us to make the critical decisions.

"We may affirm absolutely that nothing great in the world has been accomplished without passion."
Georg Wilhelm Friedrich Hegel,
1770–1831

I once worked for a CEO who was always holed up in his office. He was such a recluse that we'd only see him when he came to work, typically after the majority of the company, and when he walked out, typically before the rest of the company. He would e-mail us from just a few offices away rather than talk with us directly. He didn't know the names of anyone below the senior staff, didn't ever speak to them other than in passing with a "Good morning" or a "See you tomorrow." The group was "barely quivering protoplasm." The organization didn't have a direction, people looked at their jobs as simply occupations to pass the time and get a paycheck, and no one cared about the future of the company, its success or making a contribution. He was not successful.

So, simply do the opposite of the aforementioned CEO. Be there first and leave at the end of the day. Greet people and ask them what they are going to be doing today to make us a more successful company. Take every opportunity to sit down with your people, hear their stories and support them in their challenges. Catch them doing the right things and fuel their enthusiasm.

CARING FOR YOUR PEOPLE

"You can't wait for inspiration.
You have to go after it with a club."
Jack London,
1896–1916

Once I was in the chain of people reporting to an executive vice president (EVP) of Norwest Bank named Dan Saklad. He was one of those rare individuals who remembered people's names and something about their situation across an organization of hundreds of employees.

I had coordinated a quarterly offsite event for the Investment and Insurance division. I was placed at the entryway with this EVP and asked to greet the arriving team members and provide any support he might need. I'll never forget that evening and his ability to greet all but a few of those hundreds of employees personally. If he had met them, he had asked a personal question about their families or job, and he was able to ask about it at a future event. "Hey, Joe, how did it turn out with your son's baseball team?" Joe, with a look of amazement on his face, answered the question and then quickly joined a group of employees who were discussing their shock that someone at the top actually cared about them as human beings.

This executive's effect on the group was profound. That meeting and the days that followed were energized by his obvious caring approach to his people. I wish I were so brilliant!

I learned something from his actions. I now make my best attempt to quickly get and maintain an organizational chart of all my team members. I study the names and spend time with every team member, even if just a few minutes. During that time I am always able to pick out some personal issue—where they live, how many children they have, and whether there is anything we can do to improve the organization or work environment. There is always something, and I do my best to relate that to the name, face and job. It takes practice but it makes a difference.

JEAN SCHLEMMER—CORPORATE EXECUTIVE: *William James says, "The greatest need in a human being is the need to be appreciated." I don't think we do a good enough job. We forget to be "often delighted." This relates to both the team's recognition as well as an individual's recognition. Our company understands the power of alignment. When you have alignment, amazing things can happen. When you are compensated in an aligned fashion, when you are recognized in an aligned fashion. All of that produces true teamwork. You can produce outstanding results.*

General Baxter and I were once invited to a Texas Ranger's baseball game by a mutual acquaintance. At the pregame tailgate reception, we were introduced to former Speaker of the House Jim Wright. Now, we all know a politician like Mr. Wright has met hundreds of thousands of people over his long career. During our discussion, General Baxter mentioned he was from the Rio Grande Valley of south Texas and had lived there since his retirement from the Air Force in 1982. Mr. Wright commented, "Yes, I remember you showing up at a town meeting in McAllen. You sat a couple of rows back and asked a question about the trade situation with Mexico." We were amazed and both found a new respect for Mr. Wright. He gave us the feeling he cared enough to remember the little people.

JOHN FARRISH—CORPORATE EXECUTIVE: *I'm not sure how much impact I have on the enthusiasm of the people in my world. I believe I probably spend more time working on becoming enthusiastic myself than I do trying to figure out how to make somebody else enthusiastic. I do believe if I'm not enthusiastic, then it's phony if I'm talking to people about it. And when things get real-*

ly, really tough, I think of floating down a river in Vietnam, and this doesn't seem so tough. At other times I have to step back for a 5,000-foot point of view.

One of the best examples I can think of from a corporate point of view about getting excited is we recently started hiring 350 trust officers, private bankers and portfolio managers in a time when other firms are laying off. The enthusiasm behind it is really saying this is a time that's difficult, but is there a way to take advantage of it? Is there a way we can grow our business? Is there a way we can invest in it so two, three and four years from now we're better off? I truly believe the greatest opportunities are during difficult times. Actually I think it's tougher to get enthused when times are great.

When everybody wanted to own technology stocks and people wanted to become day traders, it was exactly the time when you should not have been doing that. In my humble point of view, there is more discipline required in great times than in tough times. And I think tough times are great opportunities.

I have some senior staff members who have moved with me to three or more companies. I appreciate their loyalty to my ideas and the challenges we've faced. If you were to ask them why they have stuck with me through times (that have been both fun and tough), you'd hear that I take care of my people. This has ties to mentors, giving credit, empowering and creating a positive atmosphere, but ends up keeping them enthusiastic about the job.

"Dare to do things worthy of imprisonment
if you mean to be of consequence."
Juvenal (Decimus Junius Juvenalis),
55–130

I've been in situations where a superior has suggested I eliminate one of my staff. In some cases, they were right on the money and the elimination was already in the works. Generally, in those cases, I didn't hear from them again as it relates to me doing my job and dealing with my personnel issues. (Actually, I find it quite demotivating to have someone tell me how to run my component of the business, so long as I'm doing an effective job. Input is fine; empowerment is critical.) In other situations, I disagreed and put my own position on the line in defense of an employee. In the most extreme example, I suggested we sell my component of the company in lieu of eliminating some of these great team members. This actually came to pass, and the team members stayed with us. In fact, some of those eliminated earlier under budget constraints were rehired.

At a later team meeting, one of those people stood in front of the company and shared what it meant to have a boss that really cared about him as a person. He is enthusiastic and hard working and has my complete support. The rest of the team, I'm certain, felt some comfort in his comments.

HALE BURR—CONSULTANT, FIGHTER PILOT AND RETIRED MAJOR GENERAL: *Surround yourself with talent. As much as possible, hire people who are better than you and don't be afraid of those who are smarter, quicker, more proficient, etc. A leader needs to foster teamwork because not many folks do great things by themselves. A leader must then have a recognition system to reward his good people. On the other hand, that leader must handle problems as they arise—don't hide them or procrastinate on taking care of bad apples. The old cliché about spending 90 percent of your time on 10 percent of the people in the group is true. (In my Air Force experience, it is less than 1 percent.)*

Be sure to support your key employees and let them know you

care about them above and beyond being a moneymaker for the company. Remember every one of your team members has a personal life and needs to be treated with respect.

MARK ANDERSON—CONSULTANT, FIGHTER PILOT AND RETIRED LIEUTENANT GENERAL: *I think about Herb Kelleher, an individual who has established the kind of atmosphere within Southwest Airlines that seems to exhibit "have fun, enjoy what you're doing, and you'll have those rewards" and hiring the kind of people who reflect that. He has made air travel fun in terms of the people working for him and the customers. In my opinion the low fares are one reason people fly Southwest but also they enjoy it despite the herdlike getting-on routine because they're on time, and they make it fun and enjoyable to be on the airplane. It all adds up to a successful operation.*

JIM PASCHALL—RANCHER, BUSINESSMAN, FIGHTER PILOT AND RETIRED LIEUTENANT COLONEL: *You've always got to be enthusiastic as a leader. When you come in every morning, you've got to come in "with your hair on fire." I'm ready to go; let's all get up and let's get after it. And you've got to show enthusiasm all the time that you're in hearing range of those you are responsible for leading. You can't slack off—ever!*

There is a certain enthusiasm that runs core to the experience I had as a fighter pilot. The spirit of the group, the pride, the mutual support, and the professionalism are without compare. While doing research for this book, I recorded many interviews with the help of video expert Steve Goranson. Steve picked up on a certain camaraderie that existed between the fighter pilots we interviewed. It all contributes to the enthusiasm you can find in a topnotch fighter squadron. At the end of the interview with General

Westbrook, Steve asked the following question. Thought you'd enjoy the response.

STEVE GORANSON—BUSINESSMAN, CORPORATE EXECUTIVE AND VIDEO EXPERT: *Fighter pilots in particular have created camaraderie unlike any other I've been around. What is it about being a fighter pilot that makes you a better officer and leader? Is there something about fighter pilots that generates a higher level of enthusiasm?*

SAM WESTBROOK—CONSULTANT, BUSINESSMAN, FIGHTER PILOT AND RETIRED BRIGADIER GENERAL: *Yes. We're all heroes! (chuckle). I think it starts with a selection process that is very tough. You end up in a situation where, number one, you have to jump over various educational hurdles to get yourself in a position where you can be considered to go off to pilot training in the military. Number two, once having done that, then you have to pass a series of physical tests that are pretty rigorous and eliminate a lot of other people. So you're already in a way setting up a little bit of an elitist society. Once you get into pilot training, you go along up to a certain point, and then there's another evaluation.*

It's almost like the British education system. First, you have passed the 11 plus (eleven grades), then pass the university exams, and if you do really well in the university exams, you get to go to Oxford or Cambridge. Otherwise you go to a red brick university or to one of the other universities. So it's a very elitist system. In other words, you get to a certain point and you've gone over these other hurdles, and then they say okay, now we know you can fly. You guys are going to fly helicopters and you guys are going to fly transports and other big heavy things. You guys, who really have the good hands and can land the airplane on "the number seven" every time at the end of the runway, are going to go become fighter pilots. There is already a little bit of elitism at that point. You've had to jump through these hoops.

But I think the other thing is once you get into fighter training, it's very intensive, it's very focused, and even though you've gone over these other hurdles, not everybody makes it through. You start out as a follower and then build your way up to a leader. A tremendous amount of skill is involved. It's almost like being on an NFL football team. You have all kinds of basic skills you need, and then you build on top of those all these other tactical and strategic skills. You do this up until the point you step out into a higher leadership position. That's your focus, and it takes a tremendous of time and effort.

You're a member of the team. You trust the other members of that team with your life because when you're flying on somebody's wing, if he flies into a mountain, you're also going to fly into a mountain. By working together all the time, and having been through all these programs, you build up camaraderie and a trust that is unusual. All of those disciplines, later on, will put you in good stead as a leader so long as you have an interest in that way.

Among fighter pilots, there are those who go through the basic stuff and get up to the point where they are an accomplished fighter pilot. They've been through most of the advanced training programs, and all they really want to do is stay in that airplane and be a fighter pilot. They don't want to go any further.

Another group of people get to that point and say "yes," I've done all this, but I'm excited enough about the idea of leading people, I want to go do that. And some of those people discover senior leadership is not really all it's cracked up to be. They may want to go back to the squadron, but usually have trouble doing that. Other people get out and say, "Yes, now I understand that, I want to keep my skills as a fighter pilot. I won't be as good as I used to be because I can't immerse myself in it, but I want to do the other stuff that goes along with leading large organizations. I want to have that opportunity."

In my opinion, the best way to understand what a fighter squadron is like is to read the first two chapters of The Right Stuff. *That's about as good a description you'll find of what it's like to be in a fighter squadron.*

Let me summarize: I think it is a combination of the screening and training program, a competitive lifestyle requiring discipline and focus, and a constitution that includes the energy and moxie needed to excel. This makes the fighter pilot community feel good about itself and generates an enthusiasm for the mission. It all translates into better officers, better leaders and a personality type that is driven to excel.

Remember, creating enthusiasm is one component necessary to build a fabulous team. It requires forethought and stamina, but can also make for a lot of fun.

To generate the proper level of enthusiasm, be sure to utilize:

- Sprints and long drives.

Remember, in order to have everyone enthusiastic about their jobs, you need:

- Input from everyone.

No one can be pumped up about a boss who doesn't show some empathy, so use:

- Walk-around management, and
- Be sure to care for your people.

CONCLUSION

"There are two ways of spreading light: to be the candle or the mirror that reflects it."
Edith Wharton,
1862–1937

Hundreds of books, with thousands of techniques, have been written about leadership. I've not read 10 percent of those books. I have, however, been fortunate to live a diverse series of leadership and management opportunities and, more important, I've worked for and with some outstanding leaders.

Leaders with more than 500 years of combined experience have contributed their best practices to this book. They have expertise that has been tested in staff positions, combat situations and the corporate world. They all have their "bag of tricks" and experiences from which we were able to draw.

I'm a firm believer in not reinventing the

Daily activities

Integrity

Excellence versus perfection

wheel, and as such, have elected to learn as much as I can from those who have gone before—those who have found and tested a myriad of leadership techniques.

HALE BURR—CONSULTANT, FIGHTER PILOT AND RETIRED MAJOR GENERAL: *I believe there are many things learned or experienced during a military career about leadership that are directly applicable to individuals and companies in the civilian world. From the beginning, young officers are trained and educated in desirable leadership characteristics and qualities such as integrity, loyalty, teamwork, discipline, setting and meeting high standards and the value of hard work.*

When I started work on this book, I had so many ideas it seemed it would take forever to put them down in words. I went back to a fundamental organizational technique and focused on three key areas: Self, Team and Atmosphere. Each of these areas is broken down into three subsets that cover, in my humble opinion, the majority of leadership challenges. Inevitably some overlap exists, but I've chosen to regard this as a good thing. The areas naturally reinforce each other and one can't exist without the other being addressed. Much like a chain, if any of the links are weak or ignored by the leader, then the chain become useless.

For those now moving into their first leadership role, you now have a foundation to build your own leadership personality. For those with years of leadership experience, I'm hoping this text has provided some reinforcement and perhaps some technique and anecdotal support.

DR. SANDRA DAVIS—CORPORATE EXECUTIVE, AUTHOR AND PSYCHOLOGIST: *Someone said to me the other day, "I think I can be most effective as a leader if I really understand my sweet spots. I want you to help me understand where my sweet spots are, and in what* *environment I can really make those soar." I think that's a question everyone in a leadership role needs to figure out for themself.*

It used to be when people looked at leadership, they'd say let's figure out if you have the right stuff. Is the person confident and resilient? Does he or she have the leadership moxie? What about executive presence? What about interpersonal skills?

That's all well and good, but in fact, leadership is also about the interaction between you and others. What all leaders have in common are followers. Not every individual can be a good leader for every team. That's also a lesson in humility. You can be really good in one situation, but you may not be as effective in another situation.

True leadership builds over time, as people understand they can trust the leader. That there is a consistency about the leader's actions and they can count on the person to make good decisions and be there when the chips are down.

Most of us quickly read through leadership texts and select one or two techniques to reinforce our current approach—arrows in our leadership quiver. These can be called upon, as needed, with the understanding every situation is going to be different from the next. I suggest you try a technique, evaluate its success and decide whether it fits your style.

We must study, assimilate and then modify when we take the technique to a real-world situation. In Air Force pilot training, classroom instruction provided the basis and was followed up and reinforced by our experiences actually flying the jets. The need for real-world experience was borne out by my pilot training class with a specific example. The Air Force had invested a significant amount of money into flight simulators. In the late '70s, the simulators provided video as well as motion and were a great improvement over the static, procedural trainers.

Our class went through all of our instrument flight training in these simulators. Previously, pilot trainees received some instruction in the simulators/trainers but also received a significant amount of flight training in the actual jet. I don't recall the precise statistic but the lack of the actual flying experience and the associated complications presented by weather, turbulence, air traffic control, vertigo and air sickness pushed our instrument check ride pass rate way down. Real-world application is different, where making mistakes and experiencing the constant changes associated with being a leader are critical.

In pilot training we were taught to memorize the procedures associated with a myriad of emergency situations. I was taught how to deal with smoke and fumes in the cockpit in the T-37 trainer. The procedure described the need to select 100 percent oxygen, depressurize the cabin and land as soon as practical. On my very first solo flight in the T-37, I had an electrical circuit short out, which I first recognized as smoke coming from under the dash. At the time, I was upside down in a loop, and there were many factors to consider.

I did not run through the printed procedure the instant I saw the smoke. I first finished my loop, thinking it would be easier to solve this problem right side up! The same holds true for application of leadership and management techniques. We need to continually order the challenges at hand, and it is likely that before we get through our original game plan, we'll be modifying them again and again. Having a bag of tricks, testing the effectiveness of those tricks and having the flexibility to modify on the fly . . . that's what we're talking about.

On my first solo flight in the T-38, I was doing aerobatics in West Texas. I noticed one of my engines had a fluctuating oil pressure that eventually went to zero. I ended up shutting off that engine and recovering to Reese Air Force Base with a single engine. Not a big deal; in fact, I enjoyed the distraction from business as usual and flew back with no complications. There was a reason they designed the airplane with two engines! There are similar reasons to have multiple responses and tools available to deal with the variables of real-life leadership.

This book contains the overview of the leadership mantra to which I refer when faced with the inevitable challenges. I'm not saying it is the catchall solution for today's emerging leaders, but it will give you the start you need to move down the road to becoming an effective leader.

Good luck!

BIOGRAPHIES

MARCUS ANDERSON

Lieutenant General Marcus Anderson retired from active duty in April 1996. Since then he has been a part-time consultant for Burdeshaw Associates, Ltd., in Bethesda, Maryland, and with the Executive Service Corps of San Antonio, a volunteer organization that supports nonprofit and publicly funded agencies in the San Antonio area.

Anderson served as National Commander of the Order of Daedalians from June 1998 to June 2001. This is a 16,000-member nonprofit organization of active duty and retired military pilots from the U.S. armed services. Also, in July 1999, he became board chair of the Association of Graduates, U.S. Air Force Academy, a 17,000-member organization that supports the Academy and the graduate community.

Anderson
Barlow
Baxter
Burr
Davis
Farrish
Fisher
Latham
Lorber
Mehlin
Paschall
Remkes
Schlemmer
Schmitt
Westbrook

From 1993 until his retirement, General Anderson was the Air Force Inspector General, Office of the Secretary of the Air Force, Washington, D.C. He was responsible for assessing the readiness, discipline and efficiency of the Air Force through inspections, management reviews, investigations and staff visits. From 1991 to 1993, he was Commander of the Air Force's Operational Test and Evaluation Center, responsible for realistic operational testing, analysis and evaluation of major weapon systems acquired by the Air Force. He oversaw Air Force inspection policy; criminal investigations; counterintelligence operations; the complaints and fraud, waste and abuse programs; intelligence oversight and two field operating agencies—the Air Force Inspection Agency and the Air Force Office of Special Investigations.

General Anderson commanded 3rd Air Force from 1988 to 1991. He was responsible for the readiness, discipline and support of over 20,000 Air Force personnel based in the United Kingdom at eight major installations with over 300 aircraft. He served as Director of Operations for Tactical Air Command from 1986 to 1988 and was responsible for the readiness and training of tactical forces based in the United States.

General Anderson was Commandant of Cadets at the Air Force Academy from 1984 to 1986 and was responsible for the military training, airmanship programs, character development and support of 4,400 cadets. From 1977 to 1984, he served successively on a NATO staff; three-plus years in an F-15 Wing, culminating as Wing Commander; and in Headquarters U.S. Air Force Europe as Assistant Director of Operations, then as Director of Plans.

From 1965 to 1977, General Anderson flew as an operational fighter pilot in the F-100 and F-4, to include combat tours in Southeast Asia. He served as a Flight Commander and later as a Squadron Commander. He attended the USAF Fighter Weapons School, the Armed Forces Staff College and the National War College.

Starting as an Air Force Academy graduate in 1961, Anderson has held a variety of operational and staff assignments including commander of a fighter wing in Europe, commandant of cadets at the academy, commander of a Numbered Air Force in Europe, and commander of the Air Force Operational Test and Evaluation Center. He was a command pilot in the F-100, F-4, F-15 and A-10 with more than 4,400 flying hours, including 240 combat missions in Southeast Asia.

Major awards and decorations include Distinguished Service Medal, Legion of Merit with oak leaf cluster, Distinguished Flying Cross, Defense Meritorious Service Medal with oak leaf cluster, Meritorious Service Medal with two oak leaf clusters, Air Medal with 13 oak leaf clusters, Air Force Commendation Medal with oak leaf cluster, Vietnam Service Medal with three service stars, and Republic of Vietnam Gallantry Cross with Palm.

He has a bachelor of science degree from the Air Force Academy, and a masters degree in systems management from the University of Southern California.

NEAL BARLOW

Colonel Neal Barlow has served as a professor and head of the Department of Aeronautics at the U.S. Air Force Academy in Colorado Springs, Colorado, since July 2000. He is responsible for the command and leadership of the academy's largest engineering department that directs the fluid and thermal sciences portion of accredited mechanical engineering education program. He is also responsible for continued development and execution of the university-level accredited aeronautical engineering education program.

Prior to assuming his present duties, Barlow served as the Air Force Academy's 34th Operations Group deputy commander and as the commander of the 94th Flying Squadron. His role was to supervise the Standardization/Evaluation Division, ensuring aircrew readiness in nine aircraft types. This operations group generates 60,000 soaring and 15,000 parachuting sorties, using 101 aircraft and 300 instructor pilots/jumpmasters to support an annual student load of 2,700 cadets. As commander of the 94th Flying Training Squadron, he was responsible for 300 officers, cadets and civilian personnel who conduct 50,000 sorties annually in glider and powered aircraft.

During summer and fall 1997, Barlow commanded the 4417th Support Squadron and served as site commander at Ali Al Salem Air Base, Kuwait. This was the most forward-based Air Force site in the Joint Task Force Southwest Asia Area of Responsibility (JTF-SWA). The Colonel was responsible for security forces, civil engineering, services, logistics, medical, and contracting and finance functions.

Colonel Barlow is a 1978 distinguished graduate of the Air Force Academy with a degree in aeronautical engineering. He received his master's of science degree in aeronautical and astronautical engineering as an Order of Daedalian Fellow from the University of Washington and a Ph.D. in aerospace engineering from Arizona State University.

Colonel Barlow is a command pilot with more than 4,000 flying hours. In his twenty-two years of instructor experience, he has served at every level of undergraduate flight training, from line instructor pilot, to PIT instructor, to command evaluator. His Air Force instructor experience includes the T-38, T-41, T-3 and T-G7 aircraft, along with civilian instructor experience in numerous aircraft types.

Personally, Colonel Barlow is assistant varsity basketball coach at the Air Academy High and a youth soccer and competitive basketball coach.

BUZ BAXTER

Walter H. Baxter, III, was born in the very southern-most tip of Texas on July 26, 1926. He was reared and schooled in his hometown of Weslaco where he joined the Texas State Guard as a private of infantry in 1942. He graduated from high school in 1943 and attended what is today the University of Texas at Arlington. He volunteered for duty in the Army Air Corps and became a P-38 mechanic before earning an appointment to the U.S. Military Academy at West Point, where he graduated June 1950.

Baxter went to flying school, was selected to become a fighter pilot and assigned to the 18th Fighter Bomber Wing in Korea. He quickly became combat ready in the F-51 Mustang, and in a short time became a flight leader, often leading squadron and even group-strength formations deep into enemy territory.

Upon completing his combat tour, he returned to the United States, remained in fighters, and upgraded to jets. Among his duties, he was to develop a mobility plan for the first threat of hostilities. The plans and procedures he produced for his squadron were adopted for the parent wing and later by the Tactical Air Command. Ultimately those mobility plans were applied to the Composite Air Strike Force and still serve as the foundation for rapid-response reaction force planning today.

Next, Baxter served in England as a pilot and wing gunnery and bombing officer before being assigned to the newly established Air Force Academy as an instructor in the Department of Military Studies. From the Academy, he went back to full-time duty in the cockpit. In fact he was never off flying status, although at various times he was director of officer training, executive officer for the wing commander, the wing disaster control officer, or a student in Air Command and Staff College.

Baxter went to Germany as a young major, and returned three years later as a colonel, having been a fighter squadron operations officer for a year, then commander for two years. He attended Army War College, flew a tour with the 8th Tactical Fighter Wing (TFW) in Southeast Asia, first as deputy commander for operations and later as deputy wing commander. A squadron of B-57Gs, with the latest in forward-looking infrared target-finding equipment, joined the four squadrons of F-4 Phantom II to make the strongest, most powerfully equipped fighter wing in the history of the USAF to that time.

After returning to the United States, he became the commander of the Pilot Training Wing in Lubbock; then served as vice commander of the Technical Training Center at Keesler AFB, Mississippi. Here he was promoted from colonel to brigadier general and almost immediately sent back to Southeast Asia. The Vietnam War was winding down, but there was still a lot to do in Thailand where bases were being closed and the local people were very anxious about their fate when their American friends were gone. Brigadier General Baxter participated in the planning and execution of U.S. personnel withdrawal from South Vietnam and Cambodia. Then he was involved in the Battle for KoTang Island and the return of the U.S. cargo ship, the Mayaguez.

Baxter moved from Thailand to Okinawa and served as commander of the 18th Fighter Wing, the unit he had first seen combat with in Korea. (In his two tours with the 18th, he wore four different insignia of rank: 2nd Lieutenant, 1st Lieutenant, Brigadier General and Major General). His next assignment was with the North American Air Defense Command where he commanded the 24th NORAD Region. Just a year later, Baxter moved from Montana to Oslo, Norway, were he served as air deputy for the commander-in-chief of Allied Forces, Northern Europe.

The NATO tours concluded with an assignment to command 3rd Air Force with headquarters in England. A year later on July 30, 1982, when the Royal Air Force Band played "The Star Spangled Banner" and "God Save The Queen," it was the culmination for General Baxter of almost 40 years of military service.

This also marked the beginning of a new career in the business world. General and Mrs. Baxter made the last of their twenty-four household moves in returning to Weslaco, Texas. His father died five months later, and General Baxter moved forward to take over the family vegetable seed business. He surrounded himself with good people, applied his leadership skills, did his homework, and in five years time, doubled sales and increased profitability three-fold. He was active in his church, became president of the Weslaco Rotary Club, served on the city airport board, joined the chamber and was elected president of the Rio Grande Valley Chamber of Commerce. He was also elected president of the Texas Vegetable Association. As the chairman of Mid Valley Bank in Weslaco, he helped engineer the merger of his bank with Texas Regional Bank, on whose board he still serves. The governor appointed him to the Texas Aviation Board, and he was appointed to the Texas Chamber of Commerce, becoming chamber vice president. He is co-founder of "Citizens Against Lawsuit Abuse," was selected to be Rio Grande Valley Man of the Year by the Boy Scouts of America, and in 2001, was named a "Distinguished Alumni of the University of Texas, Arlington." He continues to fly his Beechcraft Bonanza. Additionally, he plays golf, is a Stephen Minister and exercises four or more days each week. He and his wife, Lila, have four grown children and four grandchildren. The Baxters make their home in Fair Oaks Ranch, Texas, near San Antonio.

HALE BURR

Major General (Retired) Hale Burr has over twenty years in key leadership and executive management positions of increasing responsibility. His extensive experience is in high-level government leadership and policy-making positions, most of which involved working in a multinational environment and international military sales. Hale has created marketing strategies to develop new sales programs and to successfully obtain export licenses, technology releases and approvals from the U.S. government. His in-depth experience has been working with political and military leaders, ambassadors, high-level staff and government officials in Europe/NATO, the Middle East, Asia, Africa and Latin America.

After retiring from the Air Force in 1997, Burr has been consulting involving business continuity and recovery, strategic planning, business development and marketing, project management and technical analysis for domestic and international companies.

Military accomplishments: The general entered the Air Force in 1965 as a distinguished graduate of the Texas A&M Reserve Officer Training Corps program. He has commanded a tactical fighter squadron, a tactical training wing, a tactical fighter wing, and numbered air force, as well as served as the deputy commander for a joint task force in the Persian Gulf. He is a command pilot with more than 3,500 flying hours in fighter aircraft. He has flown more than 500 combat missions and more than 1,100 combat flying hours in the F-4 and O-2 aircraft while serving two combat tours in Southeast Asia.

As a Major General from 1994 to 1997, Burr was Principal Assistant Deputy Undersecretary of the Air Force, International Affairs. He was responsible for formulating and integrating U.S. Air Force policy in following areas: politico-military affairs, security assistance, technology release and information disclosure issues, and attaché/exchange officer programs in support of U.S. government objectives. This area managed all international programs for the Air Force that included 100 countries and over $105 billion in foreign military sales.

As Commander, 13th Air Force, U.S. Pacific Command from 1991 to 1994, Burr led all U.S. Air Forces in the largest area of responsibility for any numbered Air Force commander. He greatly improved military-to-military relations by frequent exercises and extensive travel throughout South and Southeast Asia. He also created deployable air combat capable command element to handle any contingency in the western Pacific and Indian Ocean area.

For a year, Burr was a brigadier general assigned as Deputy Director for Operations, National Military Command Center, and the Joint Chiefs of Staff. He was responsible for providing attack assessment to the National Command Authority, disseminating decisions for the employment of tactical and strategic nuclear weapons, monitoring the status of United States and friendly operational forces and providing initial direction and management to worldwide emerging crises. Throughout Desert Shield/Storm, Burr led the Pentagon crisis action team that directed the combat operations and logistic support of U.S. military forces deployed in the Middle East.

As Deputy Commander, Joint Task Force Middle East, U.S. Central Command, Burr was responsible for operational control of all U.S. military forces assigned to support tanker escort operations and other designated missions in the Persian Gulf and North Arabian Sea. He obtained extensive maritime operational experience while serving aboard the USS LaSalle, home-ported in Bahrain. He interfaced frequently with key regional political and military decision-makers.

Other assignments from 1965 to 1989 had him in various positions of responsibility in command, high-level staff, and resource management for operational flying activities including aircraft maintenance, civil engineering, installation security, communications, training and education. He developed policy and managed a $58 billion program of weapons systems, military equipment and training sales and services to fourteen countries in the Middle East and northeast Africa. This position required frequent travel and personal contact with senior foreign military and government officials. Burr commanded an F-16 and F-4 flying organization and installation of over 9,000 personnel with an annual budget in excess of $58 million and assets of $1.5 billion. He directed all F-15 and T-33 flying operations and maintenance activities including 1,800 personnel, 92 aircraft and a $200 million industrial plant.

Burr's education includes a masters of arts in international relations from the University of Arkansas and a bachelor of arts in economics, Texas A&M University. He also attended the National War College, Fort McNair, D.C.; Air War College, Maxwell Air Force

Base, Alabama; U.S. Army Command and General Staff College, Fort Leavenworth, Kansas; and National and International Security Management, Harvard University. He is a Certified Business Continuity Professional # 2650, Disaster Recovery Institute and USAF Research Associate, University of Miami.

His major awards and decorations are Distinguished Service Medal, Defense Superior Service Medal, Legion of Merit, Distinguished Flying Cross with four oak leaf clusters, Defense Meritorious Service Medal, Meritorious Service Medal with two oak leaf clusters, Air Medal with thirty-one oak leaf clusters, and Air Force Commendation Medal.

SANDRA DAVIS

Dr. Sandra Davis is a co-founder of MDA Consulting Group in Minneapolis, Minnesota, and serves as the organization's CEO. Through her consulting work, Davis focuses on the identification and growth of leadership talent and the development of organizational systems that support peak performance. She is skilled in the removal of barriers that prevent people from giving their best to their work and in building organizational systems that support change.

As CEO of MDA, Davis has gained firsthand experience about leadership and teamwork in running a business. She maintains client relationships as well. Her client work includes executive selection and coaching, succession planning, team building, cultural change and organizational development.

Davis's consulting experiences are diverse. Her in-depth knowledge of her clients' businesses helps her assist them as they create strategic plans for people and human resource systems. Under this umbrella, she has helped create talent review processes, leadership development programs, assessment centers and competency models.

Internationally known, Davis is an expert in the use of two psychological testing tools—the California Psychological Inventory

(CPI) and the Myers Briggs Type Indicator (MBTI). She has spoken at numerous national and international conferences on attracting, selecting and developing leadership talent.

Davis recently co-authored a book entitled *Reinventing Yourself: Life Planning After 50*, which focuses on individual self-evaluation and planning for the future. She also contributed a chapter in a recently published book titled *Individual Psychological Assessment*.

After completing her Ph.D. at the University of Minnesota in 1973, Davis stayed on as a faculty member. There she worked with students and faculty in the Institute of Technology, starting a national research consortium focused on women in engineering and science. Four years later she joined Personnel Decisions Inc. and with that move into consulting chose to make it her career. She served as a vice president of the firm until she left in 1981 to found MDA Consulting Group with one of her colleagues.

Davis enjoys putting her energy into community activities as well, serving on such boards as the Saint Paul Chamber Orchestra, Minnesota Center for Book Arts, Illusion Theater, Edina Kids Club, the Board of Directors of the Iowa State University Foundation and the Iowa State University Dean's Council for Liberal Arts and Sciences.

JOHN FARRISH

John R. Farrish is an executive vice president of Wells Fargo and senior managing director for the Central Division of Private Client Services (PCS). PCS provides customized financial management services for the affluent.

Based in Minnesota, Farrish has responsibility for the Central Division of PCS, which encompasses the ten states of Minnesota, North and South Dakota, Nebraska, Iowa, Wisconsin, Ohio, Indiana, Illinois and Michigan. PCS includes investment management, trust, private banking and brokerage. He is responsible for approximately 1,400 people who provide clients with investment expertise and products that serve all estate planning, investment counseling, credit and brokerage needs of the high-net-worth market.

Farrish joined Wells Fargo in January 1998 and has over thirty years of experience in the financial services industry, including positions in the field and home offices of small, medium and larger brokerage and financial planning firms. He has held positions such as broker, director of financial planning, training director, regional director, director of sales and marketing, divisional director, brokerage business manager and national sales manger.

His education includes a bachelor's degree from the University of Wisconsin, completion of a Certified Financial Planning (CFP) program, Wharton Business School Industry Program, and graduate business courses at the University of Chicago and the University of Minnesota, Carlson School of Management. He also served as an arbitrator for the National Association of Securities Dealers and the American Arbitration Association.

DAVID FISHER

David Fisher has more than twenty years of corporate management and leadership experience. He has excelled in a range of professional experiences, including starting a successful software development business, responsibilities in corporate finance and marketing for a major Fortune 500 company and as a financial consultant in the investment business.

Fisher's education credentials have uniquely qualified him in the equity and capital markets, and the rigorous quantitative analysis required in his work. He completed his graduate work in finance and economics at the University of Chicago Graduate School of Business in 1989. Fisher holds both undergraduate and advanced engineering degrees from Iowa State University and The University of Texas at Austin, respectively. His engineering studies focused in mechanical engineering, particularly energy conversion and nuclear energy.

Fisher is a financial consultant with a major national investment firm. His investment practice focuses on developing portfolios for long-term growth based on the specific risk-tolerance and financial objectives of each client. He has consistently performed in the top 10 percent among his peers.

Prior to establishing his career in the investment business, Fisher worked for Occidental Energy Ventures Corporation, a wholly owned subsidiary of Occidental Petroleum Corporation. He was responsible for all marketing activities for the firm's independent power generation business in the contiguous forty-eight states. Clients included major municipalities and Fortune 500 companies. In addition to marketing, Fisher guided the development of proforma financial statements for all projects as a basis for project finance arrangements.

Fisher has contributed significantly to his community as well. He is an active member of his church and serves on numerous boards and committees. He has served on the National Board of Directors of Sigma Phi Epsilon Fraternity and was awarded the Zollinger Award for Leadership by that organization.

JIM LATHAM

Brigadier General (Retired) Jim Latham is Director, International Business Development for Lockheed Martin Aeronautics Company in Fort Worth, Texas. He is responsible for developing the market for all company products in Northern Europe and the United Kingdom. He joined the company in January 1998 after completing a twenty-eight-year U.S. Air Force career.

Jim's last assignment in the Air Force was serving as the Assistant Deputy Undersecretary of the Air Force for International Affairs. He was responsible for formulating and integrating U.S. Air Force policy with regards to politico-military affairs, security assistance, technology and information disclosure issues and attaché affairs in support of U.S. government objectives.

Latham had been commissioned into the Air Force in March 1969 through the Reserve Officer Training Corps program. As a command pilot, he was involved with tactical fighter operations during most of his career. He flew two combat tours during the Vietnam War, flying from bases in Thailand. The general spent six months in captivity in North Vietnam as a prisoner of war, after being shot down while on a combat mission in October 1972.

Flying with the U.S. Air Force Thunderbirds starting in 1978, he was right wingman and served as operations officer, then became commander and flight leader in June 1984. He led his team through its first demonstration season in the F-16.

In June 1986 General Latham attended National War College, Fort Lesley J. McNair, Washington, D.C. and was then assigned as executive officer to the director, Defense Security Assistance Agency, Office for the Secretary of Defense, the Pentagon, Washington, D.C. In August 1989 he was assigned to the 432 Tactical Fighter Wing, Misawa Air Base, Japan, as the vice commander. He commanded the 432nd Fighter Wing from August 1990 to August 1992. General Latham was then assigned to Maxwell AFB, Alabama, where he was commandant of the Squadron Officer School.

In June 1993 he became commandant of the Air Force Reserve Officer Training Corps. In 1994 and 1995, he commanded the 20th Fighter Wing at Shaw AFB, South Carolina, and the composite wing in Saudi Arabia responsible for enforcing the no-fly zone over southern Iraq.

He was promoted to Brigadier General in August 1993 and retired in 1998.

General Latham is a command pilot with more than 5,000 total flight hours in the OV-10, F-4, T-38 and F-16. He has 383 combat missions in Southeast and Southwest Asia with 920 combat hours. His military decorations and awards include the Silver Star with oak leaf cluster, Defense Superior Service Medal, Legion of

Merit with oak leaf cluster, Distinguished Flying Cross with four oak leaf clusters, Bronze Star Medal with "V" device, Air Medal with seventeen oak leaf clusters, Purple Heart with oak leaf cluster, the Air Force Association's David Schilling Award, and the Outstanding Flying Award from the USAF Fighter Weapons Instructor Course.

JOHN LORBER

As vice president of Boeing Space and Communications (S&C) Operations in the Colorado Region, General (Retired) John Lorber oversees all S&C business in the region.

Prior to January 2001, Lorber served as vice president for international business development for Boeing S&C. He also has managed new business development of air and space early warning, command and control systems for Boeing Information and Surveillance Systems.

Military accomplishments: Before joining Boeing, Lorber spent thirty-four years in the U.S. Air Force, rising to the rank of general and commander of Pacific Air Forces at Hickam Air Force Base, Hawaii. During his command, he was responsible for activities spread over half the world, supporting 44,000 Air Force personnel serving principally in Hawaii, Alaska, Guam, South Korea and Japan. He served several tours of duty in Europe and the Asia-Pacific region.

Lorber entered the Air Force in 1964, after graduating from the U.S. Air Force Academy. He flew the F-4D fighter jet as a fast-moving forward air controller in Vietnam, commanded a fighter squadron and wing, and he was a command pilot with more than 5,000 flying hours, primarily in fighter aircraft.

In 1979, Lorber earned a master's degree in personnel management from Troy State University, Alabama, and he also graduated from the Air Command and Staff College at Maxwell Air Force Base, Alabama. In 1985, he graduated from the Air War College at Maxwell.

Among his many awards and decorations, Lorber has received

the Distinguished Service Medal, Legion of Merit and Distinguished Flying Cross with oak leaf cluster. He also was awarded Japan's Grand Cordon of the Order of the Rising Sun, First Order of Merit, and the Republic of Korea's Order of National Security Merit Tong II Medal.

RANDY MEHLIN

Lieutenant Colonel (Retired) Randall L. Mehlin retired from active duty in the U.S. Air Force in September 1991. Since his retirement, he has been a pilot for Southwest Airlines.

From 1988 until his retirement, Lieutenant Colonel Mehlin was an F-16 pilot at Misawa Air Base, Japan, where he served as operations officer and squadron commander of the 14th Tactical Fighter Squadron "Samurais" and as deputy operations group commander for the 432 Tactical Fighter Wing.

During the period 1985 to 1988, Lieutenant Colonel Mehlin was the operations officer of the 4484 Test Squadron at Tyndall Air Force Base, Florida. He flew the F-16 on operational test and evaluation missions primarily on the radar and electronic warfare suite, as well as tactics development test and evaluation on various weapons' subsystems.

He was a flight commander and chief of wing weapons and tactics in the 56 Tactical Training Wing at Mac Dill AFB, Florida, from 1982 to 1985. During this assignment, he flew the F-16 as a replacement training unit instructor pilot. He is also a graduate of the USAF Fighter Weapons School.

After graduation from the University of Nebraska and commissioning through the Reserve Officer Training Corps program, Lieutenant Colonel Mehlin attended Undergraduate Pilot Training at Webb AFB, Texas. After graduation he flew the F-4 at Hahn Air Base, Germany; Seymour-Johnson AFB, North Carolina; and Kunsan Air Base, Republic of Korea, where he was selected to convert to the F-16 as part of the initial cadre.

Lieutenant Colonel Mehlin has a master's degree from Golden

Gate University and also graduated from Air Force Squadron Officers School and Air Command and Staff College.

JIM PASCHALL

Lieutenant Colonel (Retired) Jim Paschall joined Arch Petroleum Inc. in the oil and gas industry after retiring from the Air Force in 1973. He served Arch Petroleum as vice president for operations until he retired in 1995. Paschall and his wife Janice are owners/operators of a ranch in Texas where they are engaged in a cow/calf operation. He serves as chairman of the Wise County Tax Appraisal Board and as a director/secretary of the Wise County Soil and Water Conservation District Board.

Texan Jim B. Paschall joined the Air Force in June 1952 and after becoming "of age," entered the Aviation Cadet Program, and was honored as a Distinguished Graduate from Radar Officer School at James Connelly AFB, Waco, Texas. After tours at Portland International Airport and Paine AFB, Everett, Washington, he entered Pilot Training in October 1958 at Bartow, Florida, again honored as a Distinguished Graduate.

Following a tour in the Northwest in F-89s and F-102s, Paschall served in Spain for three-and-one-half years. Upon returning to George AFB, California in 1964, he flew the F-4. After a tour at Ubon, Thailand, in 1965, he completed Fighter Weapons School as the "Outstanding Student." He departed George AFB in 1967 to attend Air Command and Staff College. Paschall then had a second tour in Southeast Asia at Udorn, Thailand. Afterwards, he served at Bitburg Air Base, Germany, as operations officer of an F-4E equipped squadron until entering Air War College in 1971. His last assignment was at Tactical Air Command Headquarters where he retired in September 1973.

Decorations include the Distinguished Flying Cross with four oak leaf clusters and the Air Medal with fifteen oak leaf clusters.

DUTCH REMKES

Brigadier General Robertus C.N. Remkes is commander of the 3rd Wing Elmendorf Air Force Base in Alaska. Prior to that, he was the deputy director of plans and programs, Headquarters Air Combat Command, Langley Air Force Base, Virginia. He was responsible for developing strategic plans and programs supporting the joint employment of Combat Air Forces (CAF). He developed and integrated CAF force structure requirements and directed planning, programming and budgeting system activities. He also provided analyses on force structure, readiness, and commander-in-chief requirements and guidance to increase efficiency using innovative principles.

The brigadier general received his commission upon graduation from the United States Air Force Academy in 1977 and completed pilot training at Reese Air Force Base, Texas, in December 1978. He has served as a squadron, group and wing commander. He has flown the F-4, F-16, T-37, T-38 and the T-1. Brigadier General Remkes is a graduate of the United States Air Force Fighter Weapons School. He is a command pilot with more than 2,600 hours of flight time.

Remkes' education is wide-ranging as follows: 1977, bachelor of science degree in history, United States Air Force Academy; 1984, Squadron Officer School, Maxwell Air Force Base, Alabama; Air Command and Staff College, correspondence; master's degree in aviation management, Embry Riddle Aeronautical University; Armed Forces Staff College, Norfolk, Virginia in 1994; and the Air War College, Maxwell Air Force Base, Alabama.

Major awards and decorations include Legion of Merit; Defense Meritorious Service Medal, Meritorious Service Medal with four oak leaf clusters, Air Medal with one oak leaf cluster, Air Force Commendation Medal with one oak leaf cluster, Air Force Achievement Medal, Air Force Outstanding Unit Award, and Air Force Organizational Excellence Award.

JEAN SCHLEMMER

Jean C. Schlemmer is executive vice president of asset management for General Growth Properties, Inc. She oversees and is responsible for the following General Growth Properties business units: three geographic groups of owned and/or joint venture partnership regional shopping centers; third-party management of regional shopping centers; business development; and redevelopment.

Schlemmer joined General Growth Properties (GGP) in 1989 when General Growth acquired The Center Companies, a Minneapolis-based shopping center management company. She held a variety of supervisory positions in leasing until she became senior vice president of asset management for fifty-five wholly owned regional malls in 1997, a position she held until she was promoted to her current role in 2000.

Schlemmer had been with The Center Companies since 1986 as vice president of leasing for the Western region and became vice president of leasing for the entire company in October 1987. Prior to joining The Center Companies, she was president of her own retail real estate company for three years. Previous to that she was in charge of leasing for both Gabbert & Beck and Cedar-Riverside Associates, Inc., in the Twin Cities.

Schlemmer has worked with the Gallup organization to foster a strengths-based leadership/management philosophy within GGP. Based on hundreds of thousands of interviews in its research on successful companies, Gallup produced two books—*First Break all the Rules* and *Now Discover Your Strengths*—that encourage companies to focus on maximizing people's strengths, rather than fixing weaknesses.

She is a member of the International Council of Shopping Centers, the Advisory Board to the Men's Athletic Department at the University of Minnesota, and the President's Club at the University of Minnesota. She is also a member of the Urban Land

Institute and has served on two ULI Advisory Studies for Anaheim, California, and Charlotte, North Carolina.

ROGER SCHMITT

Colonel Roger Schmitt, born in New Jersey, was 16 years old when he graduated from preparatory school. He attended Seton Hall University majoring in physics. In 1957 he entered flying training as an aviation cadet from the New Jersey Air National Guard. He received his wings in October 1958, graduating in the top 10 percent of his class. He went through fighter upgrade and gunnery school in the F-84F at Luke AFB, Arizona, graduating as the top student, winning both the academic and top gun awards.

In late 1959, Colonel Schmitt returned to the New Jersey Air National Guard. He worked for International Telephone and Telegraph (ITT) as a research assistant in the technical laboratories. Quickly he was selected to head up a project team involved in advanced semiconductor research.

In October 1961, his guard unit was called to active duty for the Berlin Crisis and was deployed to Chaumont Air Base, France. As the youngest pilot in the squadron, he was also the top gun, sweeping all four events in the annual turkey shoot. When his unit was released from active duty, he was one of eight junior officers selected from all National Guard units in Europe to remain on active duty. Schmitt became an instructor in the newly reconstituted 366th Tactical Fighter Wing.

In early 1965 Colonel Schmitt went through F-4 training at Davis-Monthan AFB, Arizona. Upon graduation he served as squadron weapons officer at Holloman Air Force Base. In February 1966 he volunteered for combat duty and deployed to DaNang Air Base, Republic of Vietnam. He was the first F-4 aircraft commander to complete 100 missions over North Vietnam

Colonel Schmitt returned to MacDill Air Force Base, Florida, as a replacement training unit instructor pilot. He was then selected for temporary duty at the Pentagon. He was chosen to serve as the F-4 expert on a select group of recently returned combat veterans in various weapons types who served as a sounding board to the secretary of defense. He returned to MacDill as an instructor and standardization check pilot.

Colonel Schmitt was reassigned to Elmendorf AFB, Alaska, in 1970 and remained there for four years, serving as weapons officer, flight commander and assistant operations officer. Colonel Schmitt returned to Southeast Asia in 1975, serving with the 13th TFS at Udorn Royal Thai Air Base, Thailand. He returned to Alaska in 1976 and served as services chief of Alaskan Air Command. In 1976 he was selected as a squadron operations officer and the following year was selected as commander of the 18th Tactical Fighter Squadron.

In 1978, Schmitt was assigned to Headquarters Tactical Air Command at Langley Air Force Base, Virginia, where he served as assistant, then chief of the basing division. In late 1981 he transferred to Holloman AFB, New Mexico, as assistant deputy commander for operations in the 479th Tactical Training Wing. Shortly thereafter he was elevated to deputy commander.

In 1984 Colonel Schmitt retired with twenty-four years of active duty. He is a command pilot with 418 combat hours and 5,000 total hours of military flying time.

Schmitt's post military career included time as the CEO of the Idaho Humane Society where he took an in-debt, animal shelter with seventeen employees to an award-winning, state-of-the-art $3.5 million facility with forty-five employees and a $1 million endowment.

Educational achievements include Squadron Officers School in 1967; Air Command and Staff College, 1975; bachelor of arts, University of Alaska (magna cum laude), 1977; Air War College in 1979; and Masters of Business Administration, Golden Gate University (distinguished graduate) in 1981.

During his career Colonel Schmitt was awarded among others, the Distinguished Flying Cross with oak leaf cluster, Meritorious Service Medal with two oak leaf clusters, the Air Medal with twelve oak leaf clusters, Air Force Commendation Medal with oak leaf cluster, National Defense Service Medal, Vietnam Service Medal with one Service Star, Republic of Vietnam Gallantry Cross with palm.

SAM WESTBROOK

Until his retirement June 1991, Major General Sam W. Westbrook III was deputy chief of staff for operations and readiness, Headquarters Air Training Command, Randolph Air Force Base, Texas. Westbrook was promoted to major general August 1989.

In industry: Since 1996 Westbrook has been a consultant as part of a management group doing technology transfer and commercialization workshops for inventors sponsored by the Department of Energy and the National Institute of Justice. He is also involved in proposal preparation and evaluation for several private contractors as well as grant programs sponsored by government agencies.

Three years prior, in late 1993, Westbrook was recruited as vice president and general manager for an aerospace manufacturing company (hydraulic pumps, valves, and flight control and engine actuators) trying to recover from five years of defense department budget cuts as well as a slump in commercial aviation sales. During his tenure, military sales revenues increased from $90 million in 1994 to $103 million in 1995 and past-due deliveries dropped from a high of $28 million to $5 million. This dramatic turn around in results led to the company being acquired.

In 1992, Westbrook was brought in as president of a high technology company doing contracting work for the U. S. government in the area of signal processing. His task was to arrest a downward spiral of revenue and operating profit. The company exceeded 1993 revenue, profit and cash flow targets by flattening the organization, reenergizing the rank and file, and beginning to use core technologies to spin off commercial products and broaden the customer base.

Westbrook also spent six months as a consultant and acting general manager of a scrap metal company just after the world scrap steel market started to plunge and the company was in its eighth straight month of losses. As acting general manager, he reduced operating expenses and cut losing lines of business to produce an operating profit in his second month. He also negotiated a contract with a large state refuse-derived fuel operation that, combined with a rate reduction from local utilities, carried the company through the market slump.

Education and military: Westbrook earned a bachelor of science degree from the U.S. Air Force Academy in 1963 and was commissioned as a second lieutenant in the Air Force. The general then spent three years as a Rhodes scholar at Trinity College, Oxford, England, achieving a bachelor of arts/master of arts honors degree in physics and an advanced degree in plasma physics. He completed Armed Forces Staff College in 1972 and National War College in 1980.

After completing his Rhodes scholarship program in August 1966, Westbrook completed pilot training at and was assigned as an F-111 pilot in Las Vegas, Nevada. He later served as an F-111 aircraft commander and as a weapons and tactics officer. After Armed Forces Staff College in 1971-72, the general flew the A-1 in Thailand and served in the Philippines. He returned to the F-111 and performed operational test and evaluation missions from 1973-1975.

In mid-1975 Westbrook was assigned to the Pentagon as an action officer in the Directorate of Plans. He worked on the National Security Council staff from October 1977 until July 1978, when he became the first chief of the Staff Group, where he did policy analysis in support of the Air Force Chief of Staff. His last year in Washington was spent at the National War College.

Westbrook was the deputy commander for operations for an F-111 wing at Royal Air Force Station Upper Heyford, England, from 1980–1982. The general then spent a year in Germany as director of inspection for U.S. Air Forces in Europe. In July 1983 he was assigned as vice commander of the F-111 wing at Royal Air Force Station Lakenheath, England, and he became commander of the wing in April 1984. In June 1986 he was named commandant of cadets, Air Force Academy, Colorado, where he spent three years.

The general is a command pilot with more than 2,300 flying hours, including twenty-two combat missions. His military decorations and awards include the Distinguished Service Medal with one oak leaf cluster, Legion of Merit with two oak leaf clusters, Meritorious Service Medal with oak leaf cluster, Air Medal and Air Force Commendation Medal.

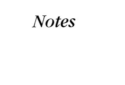

Notes

*For additional information on book orders,
speaking engagements or seminars, please visit
Bob Vosburgh's web site:*

www.9gs.org